YOU CAN WIN

Winners don't do different things.
They do things Differently.

A STEP BY STEP TOOL FOR TOP ACHIEVERS

YOU CAN WIN

Winners don't do different things.
They do things Differently.

A STEP BY STEP TOOL FOR TOP ACHIEVERS

SHIV KHERA

MACMILLAN

First Published 1998
Reprinted 1998-2002 (Twenty-five times)
Revised Edition 2002
Reprinted 2003 (thrice), 2004 (seventh)

MACMILLAN INDIA LTD
Delhi Chennai Jaipur Mumbai Patna Bangalore
Bhopal Chandigarh Coimbatore Cuttack Guwahati
Hyderabad Hubli Lucknow Madurai Nagpur
Thiruvananthapuram Visakhapatnam

Companies and representatives throughout the world

ISBN 0333 93740 6

Published by Rajiv Beri for Macmillan India Ltd.,
2/10 Ansari Road, Daryaganj, New Delhi 110 002

Printed at Sanat Printers
312, EPIP, Kundli 131 028

*To my mother
to whom I shall remain indebted
for setting the foundation
on which this book is based*

PREFACE

Success doesn't mean the absence of failures; it means the attainment of ultimate objectives. It means winning the war, not every battle.

—Edwin C. Bliss

YOU have met people who literally wander through life. They simply accept whatever fate brings them. A few may succeed by accident, but most suffer through a lifetime of frustration and unhappiness.

This book is not for them. They have neither the determination to succeed nor the willingness to devote the time and effort necessary to achieve success.

This book is for you. The simple fact that you are reading this book indicates you want to live a richer, more fulfiling life than you have now.

This book can enable you to do that.

WHAT KIND OF BOOK IS THIS?

In one sense, this book is a construction manual. It describes the tools you will need for success, and offers blueprints to help you build a successful and rewarding life.

In a second, sense, it is a cookbook. It lists the ingredients—the principles—you will need to follow to become successful and gives you the recipe for mixing them in the correct proportions.

But, above all, this is a guidebook—a step by step, how to book that will take you from dreaming about success to unlocking your potential for success.

HOW TO READ THIS BOOK

This book will help you establish new goals, develop a new sense of purpose, and generate new ideas about yourself and your future. It will enable you, as the title suggests, to guarantee yourself a lifetime of success.

But the concepts in this book cannot be absorbed by casual browsing or by gulping the whole book down in one reading. It should be read slowly and carefully, one chapter at a time. Don't move on to the next chapter until you are sure you understand every concept in the previous chapter.

Use this as a workbook. Write marginal notes to yourself. Use a highlighter as you read and mark those words or sentences or paragraphs that seem vital, or especially applicable to you.

As you read, discuss the concepts in each chapter with your spouse or partner, or with a close friend. A second (and hopefully frank) opinion from someone who knows your strengths and weaknesses can be especially helpful.

START AN ACTION PLAN

One of the purposes of this book is to help you create an Action Plan for the rest of your life. If you have never created an Action Plan, it defines three things.

1. What you want to achieve
2. How you expect to achieve it
3. When you plan to achieve it

As you read this book, keep a notebook handy, divided into three sections: your goals, the stages in which you plan to reach them, and your timetable for success.

By the time you finish reading this book, your notebook will be the foundation on which you can build your new life.

The principles in this book are universal. They are applicable in any situation, organization, or country. As Plato said, "Truths are eternal."

Throughout the book I have used masculine gender, only for the purpose of ease in writing. The principles apply to both genders and are based on the premise that most people fail not because of lack of ability or intelligence but because of lack of desire, direction, dedication, and discipline.

ACKNOWLEDGMENTS

Any accomplishment requires the effort of many people and this work is not different. I thank my daughters and especially my wife, whose patience and support was instrumental in accomplishing this task. I thank my staff whose diligent effort made this publication possible.

Many examples, stories, anecdotes are the result of a collection from various sources, such as newspapers, magazines, other speakers, and seminar participants, over the last 25 years. Unfortunately, sources were not always noted or available; hence, it became impractical to provide an accurate acknowledgment. Regardless of the source, I wish to express my gratitude to those who may have contributed to this work, even though anonymously.

Every effort has been made to give credit where it is due for the material contained herein. If inadvertently we have omitted giving credit, future publications will give due credit to those that are brought to the author's attention.

Grateful acknowledgment is made to the following for permission to use copyrighted material:
The Best of ... Bits & Pieces, copyright © 1994. Reprinted by permission. The Economics Press, Inc., 12 Daniel Road, Fairfield, NJ 07004-2565, USA. Tel: (+1973) 2271224, Fax: (+1973) 2279742, e-mail: info@epinc.com, Web-site: http://www.epinc.com

CONTENTS

1

IMPORTANCE
OF
ATTITUDE

Building a positive attitude

 There was a man who made his living selling balloons at a fair. He had balloons of many different colors, including red, yellow, blue, and green. Whenever business was slow, he would release a helium-filled balloon into the air. When the children saw the balloon go up, they all wanted one. They would come up to him, buy a balloon and his sales would go up. All day, he continued to release a balloon whenever the sales slowed down. One day, the balloon man felt someone tugging at his jacket. He turned around and a little boy asked, "If you release a black balloon, would that also fly?" Moved by the boy's concern, the man replied gently, "Son, it is not the color of the balloon, it is what's inside that makes it go up."

THE same principle applies to our lives: It's what's inside that counts. And what's inside of us that makes us go up is our attitude. William James of Harvard University said, *"The greatest discovery of my generation is that human beings can alter their lives by altering their attitudes of mind."*

YOUR ATTITUDE CONTRIBUTES TO SUCCESS

A study attributed to Harvard University found that when a person gets a job or a promotion, 85% of the time it is because of his *attitude,* and only 15% of the time because of intelligence and knowledge of specific facts and figures. It is surprising that almost 100% of education dollars go to teach facts and figures, which account for only 15% of success in life!

YOU CAN WIN is all about that 85% of success. *Attitude* is the most important word in the English language. It applies to every sphere of life, including one's personal and professional life. Can an executive be a good executive without a good attitude? Can a student be a good student without a good attitude? Can parents, teachers, salespersons, employers, or employees be good in their roles without a good attitude?

The foundation of success, regardless of your chosen field, is *attitude.*

If attitude is such a critical factor in success, shouldn't you examine your attitude towards life and ask how your attitude will affect your goals?

ACRES OF DIAMONDS

Hafiz was a farmer in Africa who was happy and content. He was happy because he was content. He was content because he was happy. One day a wise man came to him and told him about the glory of diamonds and the power that goes along with them. The wise man said, "If you had a diamond the size of your thumb, you could buy your own city. If you had a diamond the size of your fist, you could probably own your own country." And then the wise man left. That night, Hafiz couldn't sleep. He was unhappy and he was discontented. He was unhappy because he was discontented and discontented because he was unhappy.

The next morning Hafiz made arrangements to sell his farm, took care of his family, and went off in search of diamonds. He looked all over Africa and couldn't find any. He looked all through Europe and couldn't find any. By the time he got to Spain, he was emotionally, physically, and financially depleted. He was so disheartened that he committed suicide by throwing himself into the Barcelona River.

Back home, the person who had bought his farm was watering the camels at the stream that ran through the property. Across the stream, the rays of the morning sun hit a stone and made it sparkle like a rainbow. He thought the stone would look good in his living room. He picked up the stone and put it on his mantle piece. That afternoon, the wise man came and saw the stone sparkling. He asked, "Is Hafiz back?" The new owner said, "No, why do you ask?" The wise man said, "Because that is a diamond. I recognize one when I see one." The man said, "No, that's just a stone I picked up from the stream. Come I'll show you. There are many more." They went and picked some samples and sent them for analysis. Sure enough, the stones were diamonds. They found that the farm was indeed covered with acres of diamonds.*

What is the moral of this story?
There are six morals:

1. When our attitude is right, we realize that we are all walking on acres and acres of diamonds. Opportunity is always under our feet. We don't have to go anywhere. All we need to do is recognize it.
2. The grass always looks greener on the other side.
3. While we are eyeing the grass on the other side, there are others who are eyeing the grass on our side. They would be happy to trade places with us.
4. People, who don't know how to recognize opportunity, complain of noise when it knocks.
5. Opportunities are easier recognized when they are leaving rather than when they are coming.
6. Opportunity only knocks once. The next one may be better or worse, but never the same one. That is why it is so crucial to make the right decision at

---

*Adapted from Russell Cornwell, *Acres of Diamonds*. Cornwell founded Temple University based on this lecture.

the right time. A right decision at the wrong time becomes a wrong decision.

DAVID AND GOLIATH

We all know the Biblical story of David and Goliath. Goliath was a giant of a man. He struck fear in everyone's heart. One day, a 17-year-old shepherd boy came to visit his brothers and asked. "Why don't you stand up and fight the giant?" The brothers were terrified of Goliath and they replied. "Don't you see he is too big to hit?" But David said, "No, he is not too big to hit, he is too big to miss." The rest is history. We all know what happened. David killed the giant with the slingshot. Same giant, different perceptions.

Our attitude determines how we look at a setback. To a positive thinker, attitude can be a stepping-stone to success. To a negative thinker, it can be a stumbling block. Napoleon Hill, author of *Think and Grow Rich*, as well as many others have said that every problem comes with an equal or greater opportunity.

THE IMPORTANCE OF ATTITUDE TO ORGANIZATIONS

Have you ever wondered why some individuals, organizations, or countries are more successful than others? It is not a secret! They are successful because they think and act more effectively. They do so by investing in their most valuable asset—*people*.

I have spoken to executives in major corporations all over the world and asked them a question: "If you had a magic wand and there was one thing you could change that would give you a cutting edge in the marketplace, increase productivity and profits, what would that be?" Their answers were unanimous. They said they would like to change their people's attitudes. With better attitudes people would be better team players, cut back on waste and become more loyal. In general, their company would be a great place to work in.

Experience has shown that human resource is the most valuable asset of any business. People are more valuable than capital or equipment. Unfortunately, human resource is also the most wasted of resources. *People can be your biggest asset or your biggest liability.*

TQP — TOTAL QUALITY PEOPLE

Having attended a number of training programs such as customer service, selling skills and strategic planning; I have come to the conclusion that most of these are great programs with one major challenge: None of them will work unless they have the right foundation, and the right foundation is **TQP**. What is **TQP**? **Total Quality People** are people with character, integrity, good values, and positive attitudes.

Don't get me wrong. You do need the other programs, but they will only work when you have the right foundation—**Total Quality People.** For example, some customer service programs teach participants to say "please" and "thank-you," and give smiles and handshakes. But how long can a person smile if he does not have the desire to serve? Besides, people can always see through a fake smile. When the smile is not sincere, it is irritating. My point is, there has to be substance over form, not form over substance. Without a doubt, people who serve customers should say, "please" and "thank-you," smile, and so forth—these things are important. But keep in mind that they come a lot easier when accompanied by a desire to serve.

Someone once approached Blaise Pascal, the famous French philosopher, and said, "If I had your brains, I would be a better person," Pascal replied, "Be a better person and you will have my brains."

Great organizations are not measured by wages and working conditions, they are measured by feelings, attitudes and relationships. When employees say, "I can't do it," there can be two possible meanings. Either they are saying they don't know *how to* or they are saying they *'don't want to'*. If they are saying that *they don't know how to*, it is a technical training issue. If they are saying that *they don't want to*, it may be an attitude issue (they don't care), or a value issue (they don't believe they should do it).

The Calgary Tower stands at 190.8 meters. The total weight of the tower is 10,884 tons, of which 6,349 tons are below ground (approximately 60%). This shows that some of the greatest buildings have the strongest foundations. Just like a great building stands on a strong foundation, so does success. And the foundation of success is *attitude.*

A HOLISTIC APPROACH

I believe in a holistic approach. We are not just arms and legs, eyes and ears, a heart and a brain, but a complete human being. The whole person goes to work and the whole person comes home. We take family problems to work and work problems to the family. What happens when we take family problems to work? Our stress level goes up and our productivity comes down. Similarly, work problems too have an impact not only on our family but on every aspect of our lives. Personal, professional and social problems impact each other.

FACTORS THAT DETERMINE YOUR ATTITUDE

Let me ask you: Are we born with attitudes or do we develop them as we mature? What are the factors that form our attitudes? If you have a negative outlook on life because of your environment, can you change your attitude?

Most of our attitudes were shaped during our formative years.

While we were born with tendencies toward temperaments, there are three factors that largely determine our attitude formation. These are the triple E's of attitude:

1. environment
2. experience
3. education.

Let's evaluate each of these factors individually.

Environment

Environment consists of the following:

- Home: positive or negative influences
- School: peer pressure
- Work: supportive or over-critical supervisor

- Media: television, newspapers, magazines, radio, movies
- Cultural background
- Religious background
- Traditions and beliefs
- Social environment
- Political environment

All these environments create a culture. Every place—be it a home, organization, or a country—has a culture. For example, you've probably been to a store where you found managers to sales clerks alike to be polite, helpful, friendly and cheerful. Yet at another shop you find the staff rude and discourteous.

You go to a home and find the parents and children well-behaved, courteous and considerate. You go to another home where everyone is fighting like cats and dogs.

In countries where the government and political environment is honest, generally you will find that the people are honest, law abiding and helpful. And the reverse is true too. In a corrupt environment, an honest person has a hard time. Where as in an honest environment, a corrupt person has a tough time. *"In a positive environment, a marginal performer's output goes up. In a negative environment, a good performer's output goes down."*

Culture in any place always goes from the top down, never from the bottom up. We need to step back and look at what kind of environment we have created for ourselves and those around us. It is tough to expect positive behavior in a negative environment. In societies where lawlessness becomes the law, honest citizens become cheats, crooks and dacoits.

Take some time to evaluate how the environment that you are in affects you, and the one you create affects others.

Experiences

Our behavior changes according to our experiences with various people. If we have a positive experience with a person, our attitude towards him is likely to be positive and conversely negative experiences tend to make us cautious. Experiences and events become reference points in our lives, we draw conclusions which serve as guidelines for the future.

Education

Education refers to both formal and informal education. We are drowning in information but starving for knowledge and wisdom. Strategically applied, knowledge translates into wisdom which in turn translates into success.

The role of the educator is vital. A teacher affects eternity. The ripple effect is immeasurable.

Education ought to teach us not only how to make a living but also how to live.

HOW DO YOU RECOGNIZE PEOPLE WITH A POSITIVE ATTITUDE?

Just as the absence of ill health does not equal good health, in the same way the absence of negativity does not make a person positive.

People with positive attitudes have certain personality traits that are easy to recognize. They are caring, confident, patient, and humble. They have high expectations of themselves and others. They anticipate positive outcomes.

A person with a positive attitude is like a fruit of all seasons. He is always welcome.

THE BENEFITS OF A POSITIVE ATTITUDE

There are many advantages to having a positive attitude. The advantages are easy to see. But what is easy to see is also easy to miss!

A positive attitude:

Benefits for you:
- Makes for a pleasing personality
- Is energizing
- Increases your enjoyment of life
- Inspires others around you
- Helps you become a contributing member of society and an asset to your country.

And for the organization:
- Increases productivity
- Fosters teamwork
- Solves problems
- Improves quality
- Makes for a congenial atmosphere
- Breeds loyalty
- Increases profits
- Fosters better relationships with employers, employees and customers
- Reduces stress

THE CONSEQUENCES OF A NEGATIVE ATTITUDE

Life is an obstacle course and we become our biggest obstacle by having a negative attitude. People with negative attitudes have a hard time keeping friendships, jobs, marriages, and relationships. Negative attitudes lead to:

- Bitterness
- Resentment
- A purposeless life
- Ill health
- High stress levels for themselves and others.

Negative attitudes create an unpleasant environment at home, at work and become a liability to society. They pass on their negative behavior to others around them and to the future generations.

WHEN WE BECOME AWARE OF OUR NEGATIVE ATTITUDE, WHY DON'T WE CHANGE?

Human nature generally resists change. Change is uncomfortable. Regardless of its positive or negative effect, change can often be stressful. Sometimes we get so comfortable with our negativity that even when the change is for the better, we don't want to accept it. We stay with the negative.

Charles Dickens wrote about a prisoner who was locked up for many years in a dungeon. After serving his sentence, he got his freedom. He was brought out from his cell into the bright daylight of the open world. This man looked all around and after a few moments was so uncomfortable with his newly acquired freedom that he asked to be taken back to the confines of his cell. To him, the dungeon, the chains and the darkness were more familiar, secure and comfortable than accepting the change of freedom and an open world.

Many modern-day prisoners do the same thing. The stresses of having to cope in an unfamiliar world are so great that they may purposefully commit another crime in order to be sent back to prison; where, though their freedom is restricted, they have fewer decisions to make.

If your attitude is negative, your life is restricted. Your success at work will be limited. You will have fewer friends. Your enjoyment of life will be less. In the next chapter, I'll share with you my thoughts on how you can build a positive attitude. Believe me, working to build a positive attitude will be worth enduring the temporary stress and uncertainty of change.

ACTION PLAN

Dreams are a dime a dozen... it's their execution that counts.

— Theodore Roosevelt

1. List two problems you have. Then write down at least one potential positive outcome from each of the problems. Warning: This is not easy for most people. Most of us are not used to looking for opportunities in problems:

Problem	Potential benefit(s)
Problem	Potential benefit(s)

2. Practice this strategy with future problems you may encounter.

2

HOW TO BUILD A POSITIVE ATTITUDE

*Any fact facing us is not as important as our attitude
towards it, for that determines our success or failure.*

— Norman Vincent Peale

DURING childhood, we form attitudes that last a
lifetime. Undoubtedly, it would be easier to acquire
a positive attitude during our formative years. If the
combination of your inborn temperament and your early
childhood experiences have produced a positive
attitude, you are indeed very fortunate. But, if you have
acquired a negative attitude, whether by design or by
default—are you stuck with it? Of course not. Can you
change? Yes. Is it easy? Absolutely not! Is it worth it?
You bet!

How do you build and maintain a positive attitude?

- Become aware of the principles that build a positive
  attitude.
- Desire to be positive.
- Cultivate the discipline and dedication to practice
  those principles.

As adults, regardless of our environment, education
and experience, who is responsible for our attitude? We
are. We have to accept responsibility for our behavior
and actions. Some people blame everyone and everything but themselves. It is up to us to choose our attitude
every morning.

People with negative attitudes often blame the whole
world—their parents, teachers, spouse, bosses, the stars,
fate, luck, the economy and the government—for their
failures.

You have to get away from the past. Dust yourself off
and get back into the mainstream. Put your dreams
together and move forward. Thinking of the positive

things that are true, honest and good, will put you in a positive state of mind.

8 STEPS TO ATTITUDE CHANGE

If you want to build and maintain a positive attitude, you need to consciously practice the following steps:

Step 1: Change Focus, Look for the Positive

You need to become a seeker of good. You need to focus on the positive in your life. Start looking for what is right in a person or situation instead of looking for what is wrong. Because of our conditioning, most of us are so attuned to finding fault and looking for what is wrong that we often forget to see the positive picture.

LOOK FOR THE GOLD

Andrew Carnegie came to America from Scotland as a young boy. He started out by doing odd jobs and ended up as one of the largest steel manufacturers in United States. At one time, he had 43 millionaires working for him. A million dollars is a lot of money today, but in the 1920s it was worth much more.

Someone once asked Mr. Carnegie how he dealt with people. Andrew Carnegie replied, "Dealing with people is a lot like digging for gold: When you go digging for an ounce of gold you have to move tons of dirt. But when you go digging, you don't go looking for the dirt, you go looking for the gold."

Andrew Carnegie's reply has a very important message. Though sometimes it may not be apparent there is something positive in every person and every situation. We have to dig deep to look for the positive.

What is your focus? Search for the gold. If you are looking for what is wrong with people or with things, you will find many faults. What are we looking for? Gold or dirt? Even in paradise, fault finders will find faults. Most people find what they are looking for.

SOME PEOPLE WILL ALWAYS LOOK FOR THE NEGATIVE

Negative People will Always Criticize

Some people criticize no matter what. It does not matter how well something is done, they will always find fault with it. They have made a career out of criticizing. They are "career critics". They criticize as if they will win a prize at a contest. They will find fault with every person and every situation. You will find people like this in every family and office. They go around finding fault and telling everybody how bad things are and blaming the whole world for their problems. These people are energy suckers. They will go to the cafeteria and drown themselves in 20 cups of tea and coffee and smoke to their hearts' content with one excuse—they are trying to relax. All that they are doing is causing more tension for themselves and for others around them. They spread negative messages like a plague and create an environment conducive to negative results.

Robert Fulton invented the steamboat. He displayed his new invention on the banks of the Hudson River. Among the crowd who had gathered around to observe the steam boat were some pessimists and skeptics. They commented that it would never start. But lo and behold, it did. As it made its way down the river, the pessimists who said it would never start, saw it start, immediately shouted now it would never stop. What an attitude!

 There was a hunter who bought an amazing bird dog. This one-of-a-kind dog could walk on water. The hunter was looking forward to showing off his new acquisition to his friends. He invited a friend to go duck hunting. After some time, they shot a few ducks and the man ordered his dog to fetch the birds. All day long, whenever there were birds to be fetched, the dog ran on water to retrieve the birds. The owner was expecting his friend to comment or compliment him about this amazing dog, but never got one. As they were returning home, he asked his friend if he had noticed anything unusual about his dog. The friend replied, "Yes, in fact, I did notice something unusual. Your dog can't swim."

Some people always look at the negative side. Who is a pessimist? Pessimists:

- are unhappy when they have no troubles to speak of
- feel bad when they feel good, for fear they will feel worse when they feel better
- spend most of their life at complaint counters
- always turn out the lights to see how dark it is
- are always looking for cracks in the mirror of life
- stop sleeping in bed when they hear that more people die in bed than anywhere else
- cannot enjoy their health because they think they may be sick tomorrow
- not only expect the worst but make the worst of whatever happens
- don't see the doughnut, only the hole
- believe that the sun shines only to cast shadows
- forget their blessings and count their troubles
- know that hard work never hurts anyone but believe "why take a chance?"

Caution: Looking for the positive does not necessarily mean overlooking faults.

Be an Optimist

How can one be an optimist? It is well described by the following:

"Be so strong that nothing can disturb your peace of mind. Talk health, happiness, and prosperity to every person you meet. Make all your friends feel that you appreciate their good qualities and strengths. Look at the sunny side of everything. Think only of the best, work only for the best, and expect only the best. Be as enthusiastic about the success of others as you are about your own. Forget the mistakes of the past and press on to the greater achievements of the future. Give everyone a smile. Spend so much time improving yourself that you have no time left to criticize others. Be too big for worry and too noble for anger."*

Step 2: Make a Habit of Doing It Now

> *He slept beneath the moon*
> *He basked beneath the sun*
> *He lived a life of going to do*
> *and died with nothing done.*

> — James Albery

We have all procrastinated at some time in our lives. I know I have, only to have regretted it later. Procrastination leads to a negative attitude. The habit of pro-

---

* "Creed for Optimists" by Christian D. Larsen, in *The Best of … Bits & Pieces*, Economics Press, Fairfield, NJ, 1994, p. 3.

crastination fatigues you more than the effort it takes to do it.

A completed task is fulfilling and energizing; an incomplete task drains energy.

If you want to build and maintain a positive attitude, get into the habit of living in the present and doing it now.

When I Become a Big Boy

This is like the little boy who says when he becomes a big boy, he will do this and that and will be happy. And when he becomes a big boy he says that when he finishes college he will be happy. And when he finishes college he says that when he gets his first job he will be happy. And when he gets his first job he says that when he gets married, then he will be happy. And when he gets married he says when the kids get out of school he will be happy. And when the kids get out of school, he says that when he retires, he will be happy. And when he retires, what does he see? He sees life has just gone by in front of his eyes.

Some people practice procrastination by hiding behind high-sounding words, saying "I'm analyzing" and six months later they are still analyzing. What they don't realize is that they are suffering from a disease called: *Paralysis by Analysis* and they will never succeed.

Then there is another breed of people who procrastinate by saying "I'm getting ready." A month later they are still getting ready and six months later they are still getting ready. What they don't realize is they are suffering from a disease called "Excusitis." They keep making excuses.

Live in the Present

Life is not a dress rehearsal. I don't care what philosophy you believe in—we have got only one shot at this game called life. The stakes are too high to waste your life. The stakes are the future generations.

What time is it and where are we? The answer is now and we are here. Let's make the best of now and utilize the present to the fullest. The message is not that we don't need to plan for the future. The message is that we *do* need to plan for the future. If we utilize our present to its fullest, we are sowing the seeds for a better future.

If you want to build a positive attitude, learn the phrase, "do it now" and stop the habit of procrastination.

The saddest words in life are:

- "It might have been."
- "I should have."
- "I could have."
- "I wish I had."
- "If only I had given a little extra."

Never leave till tomorrow, which you can do today.

— Benjamin Franklin

I am sure all winners wanted to be procrastinators but never got around to it.

When people say, "I will do it one of these days," you can be sure it means none of these days.

Some people keep waiting for all the lights to turn green before they leave home. That will never happen. They fail even before they start. That is sad.

Stop procrastinating: Isn't it time that we put off putting things off?

Step 3: Develop an Attitude of Gratitude

Count your blessings, not your troubles. Take time to smell the roses. It is not uncommon to hear that someone, because of an accident, became blind or paralyzed, but won a million dollars in a settlement. How many of us would like to trade places with that person? Not many. We are so focused on complaining about things we do not have that we lose sight of the things we have. There is a lot to be thankful for.

When I say count your blessings, not your troubles, I don't mean that you should become complacent. Attitude of gratitude does not mean complacency. If complacence was the message you got, then I would be guilty of faulty communication and you of selective listening.

To give you an example of selective listening, let me share with you a story I heard about a medical doctor who was invited as a guest speaker to address a group of alcoholics. He wanted to make a demonstration that would be powerful enough to make people realize that alcohol was injurious to their health. He had two containers, one with pure distilled water and one with pure alcohol. He put an earthworm into the distilled water and it swam beautifully and came up to the top. He put another earthworm into the alcohol and it disintegrated in front of everyone's eyes. He wanted to prove that this was what alcohol did to the insides of our body. He asked the group what the moral of the story was and one person from behind said, "If you drink alcohol you won't have worms in your stomach." Was that the message? One course not. That was selective listening—we hear what we want to hear and not what is being said.

Many of our blessings are hidden treasures—count your blessings and not your troubles.

Step 4: Get into a Continuous Education Program

Let's get some myths out of the way. It is a general belief that we get educated in schools and colleges. During my seminars in many different countries there is a question I often ask my audience, "Do we really get educated in schools and colleges?" Generally, there is a consensus that some people do but most don't. Don't get me wrong. We receive a lot of information in schools and colleges. We do need information to be educated. But we also need to know the true meaning of education.

Intellectual education influences the head and values-based education influences the heart. In fact, education that does not train the heart can be dangerous. If we want to build character in our offices, homes and society, we must achieve a minimum level of moral and ethical literacy. Education that builds fundamental traits of character—such as honesty, compassion, courage, persistence and responsibility—is absolutely essential.

We don't need more academic education; we need more value-based education. A person who is morally educated will be a lot better equipped to move up in life or succeed than will a morally bankrupt person, with excellent academic qualifications.

Education without Values

Universities are turning out highly skilled barbarians because we don't provide a framework of values to young people, who more and more are searching for it.

— Steven Muller, President, Johns Hopkins University

True education is training of both the head and the heart. An uneducated thief may steal from the freight car but an educated one may steal the entire railroad. We need to compete for knowledge and wisdom and not for grades. Knowledge is piling up facts, wisdom is simplifying it. One could have good grades and a degree and still not learn much. The most important thing one can learn is to "learn to learn." People confuse education with the ability to memorize facts. Educating the mind without morals creates a maniac in society.

Knowledge is Not Power

We often are told that knowledge is power. Not really. Knowledge is information. It is potential power and it becomes power only when it is acted upon.

What is the difference between a person who cannot read and a person who can, but does not read? As Ben Franklin said, "Not a whole lot."

Learning is a lot like eating. It is not how much you eat that matters, what matters is how much you digest.

Knowledge is potential power; wisdom is real power.

Education takes many forms; it is not just grades and a degree. It is:

- Cultivating your strength
- Learning self-discipline
- Listening
- Eagerness to learn

Our minds are like muscles, stretch or shrink, it all depends on how much or how little we exercise them.

If you think education is expensive, try ignorance.

— Derek Bok

EDUCATION DOES NOT MEAN GOOD JUDGMENT

There is a story about a man who sold hotdogs by the roadside. He was illiterate, so he never read newspapers. He was hard of hearing, so he never listened to the radio. His eyes were weak, so he never watched television. But enthusiastically, he sold lots of hotdogs. His sales and profit went up. He ordered more meat and got himself a bigger and a better stove. As his business was growing, the son, who had recently graduated from college, joined his father.

Then something strange happened. The son asked, "Dad, aren't you aware of the great recession that is coming our way?" The father replied, "No, but tell me about it." The son said, "The international situation is terrible. The domestic situation is even worse. We should be prepared for the coming bad times." The man thought that since his son had been to college, read the papers and listened to the radio, he ought to know and his advice should not be taken lightly. So the next day, the father cut down his order for the meat and buns, took down the sign and was no longer as enthusiastic. Very soon, fewer and fewer people bothered to stop at his hotdog stand. And his sales started coming down rapidly. The father said to his son, "Son, you were right. We are in the middle of a recession. I am glad you warned me ahead of time."

What morals can we take away from this story?

1. Our expectations can create a self-fulfilling prophecy.
2. Many times we confuse intelligence with good judgment.
3. A person may have high intelligence but poor judgment.
4. Choose your advisers carefully but use your own judgment.

5. A person can, and will be, successful with or without formal education if they have the 5 Cs:

- character
- commitment
- conviction
- courtesy
- courage

6. The tragedy is that there are many walking encyclopedias who are living failures.

Intelligence is quickness to learn. Skill is an ability. Competence is the ability alongwith the willingness and desire to apply what is learned. Desire is the attitude that makes a skillful person competent. Many skillful people are incompetent. Ability without the right attitude is wasted.

The first duty of a university is to teach wisdom, not trade; character, not technicalities.

— Winston Churchill

What Does it Mean to Be Educated

Whom, then, do I call educated?

First, those who manage well the circumstances which they encounter day by day; and those who can judge situations appropriately as they arise and rarely miss the suitable course of action.

Next, those who are honorable in their dealings with all men, bearing easily what is unpleasant or offensive in others, and being as reasonable with their associates as is humanly possible.

Furthermore, those who hold their pleasures always under control and are not unduly overcome by their misfortunes, bearing up under them bravely and in a manner worthy of our common nature.

Most important of all, those who are not spoiled by their successes, who do not desert their true selves, but hold their ground steadfastly as wise and sober-minded men, rejoicing no more in the good things that have come to them through chance than in those which through their own nature and intelligence are theirs since birth.

Those who have a character which is in accord, not with one of these things, but with all of them, these are educated— possessed of all the virtues.

— Socrates (470-399 B.C.)

In a nutshell, educated persons are those who choose wisely and courageously under any circumstances. If they choose between wisdom over foolishness, good over bad, virtue over vulgarity, regardless of the academic degrees they have, then they are educated.

What is a Broad-Based Education?

Some animals in a forest decided to start a school. The students included a bird, a squirrel, a fish, a dog, a rabbit and a mentally retarded eel. A board was formed to determine the curriculum and it was decided that flying, tree climbing, swimming, and burrowing would give a broad-based education. All animals were required to take all subjects.

The bird was excellent at flying and was getting A's but when it came to burrowing, it kept breaking its beak and wings and started failing. Pretty soon, it started making C's in flying and, of course, in tree climbing and swimming it was getting F's. The squirrel was great at tree climbing, but was failing in swimming. The fish was the best swimmer but couldn't get out of the water and thus got F's in everything else. The dog didn't join the school, stopped paying taxes, and kept fighting with the administration to include barking as part of the curriculum. The rabbit got A's in burrowing but tree climbing was a real problem. It kept falling and landing on its head, suffered brain damage, and soon couldn't even burrow properly and got C's in that too.

The mentally retarded eel, who did everything half as well, became the valedictorian of the class. The board was happy because everybody was getting a broad-based education.

A true broad-based education prepares students for life, without losing their areas of specialization and competence.

We are All Gifted with Some Strengths

The small size of the hummingbird, weighing only a tenth of an ounce, gives it the flexibility to perform complicated maneuvers, such as beating its wings 75 times a second. This enables the hummingbird to drink nectar from flowers while hovering, but it cannot soar, glide or hop. The ostrich, at 300 pounds, is the largest bird, but it can't fly. However, its legs are so strong that it can run at up to 50 miles per hour, taking strides of 12-15 feet.

Ignorance

Being ignorant is not so much a shame as being unwilling to learn to do things the right way.

— Benjamin Franklin

The illusion of knowledge is not education, but ignorance. Foolish people have a strange kind of confidence which comes only with ignorance.

There is nothing wrong with ignorance, but making a career out of it is stupidity. Some people accumulate ignorance and then confuse it with education. Ignorance is not bliss. It is misery, tragedy, poverty and sickness. If ignorance is bliss, why aren't more people happy? If a little knowledge is dangerous, so is a lot of ignorance, which leads to pettiness, fear, dogmatism, egotism and prejudice. Wisdom is nothing more than dispelling ignorance.

We live in an information age. It is estimated that the amount of information is doubling every year. With information so readily available, it is easy to dispel ignorance. It is sad to see that we are taught everything but the most essential things. We are taught the three Rs (reading, riting, rithmetic), but what good is intellectual education without understanding human dignity and compassion?

Schools are a fountain of knowledge: some students come to drink, some to sip and others just to gargle.

Commonsense

We are born with five senses—touch, taste, sight, smell and hearing. But successful people have a sixth sense—Commonsense. Commonsense is the ability to see things as they are and do them as ought to be done. The application of education and knowledge without commonsense is meaningless.

Commonsense may not necessarily be a result of education. The best education without commonsense is worthless. An abundance of commonsense is called wisdom.

SHARPEN YOUR AXE

John, a woodcutter, worked for a company for five years but never got a raise. The company hired Bill and within a year he got a raise. Then John resented Bill's getting a raise after only a year and went to his boss to talk about it. The boss said, "You are still cutting the same number of trees you were cutting five years ago. We are a result-oriented company and would be happy to give you a raise if your productivity goes up." John went back, started hitting harder and putting in longer hours but he still wasn't able to cut more trees. He went back to his boss and told him his dilemma. The boss told John to go talk to Bill. "Maybe there is something Bill knows that you and I don't." John asked Bill how he managed to cut more trees. Bill answered, "After every tree I cut, I take a break for two minutes and sharpen my axe. When was the last time you sharpened your axe?"

When was the last time you sharpened your axe? Past glory and education don't count for much. We have to continuously sharpen the axe.

Feed Your Mind

Just as our bodies need good food every day, our minds need good thoughts every day. The key words in the preceding sentence are *good* food and *good* thoughts. If we feed our body with junk food and our mind with bad thoughts, we will have both a sick body and a sick mind. We need to feed our mind with the pure and the positive to stay on track.

Education is a Reservoir

Continuous positive education leads to positive thinking.

Positive thinkers are like athletes who, through practice, build an inner reservoir of stamina that they draw on during competition. If they don't practice, they have nothing to draw on.

Similarly, positive thinkers regularly build a reserve of positive attitudes by constantly feeding their mind on the pure, the powerful and the positive on a daily basis. They realize that we are all going to be faced with the negative and if we have the reserve of positive attitudes we will be able to overcome it; otherwise the negative will prevail.

Positive thinkers are not fools and they are not going through life with blinders. They are winners who *recognize their limitations,* but *focus on their strengths.* Losers, on the other hand, recognize their strengths but focus on their weaknesses.

Step 5: Build a Positive Self-Esteem

What is Self-Esteem?

Self-esteem is the way we feel about ourselves. When we feel good within, our performance goes up and our relationships improve both at home and at work. The world looks nicer. What could be the reason? Because there is a direct correlation between our feelings and behavior.

How Do We Build Positive Self-Esteem?

If you want to build a positive self-esteem quickly, one of the fastest way is to do something for those who cannot repay you in cash or kind.

 A few years ago I started volunteering my time to teach attitude and self-esteem programs to jail inmates. In just a few weeks, I learnt more than I had learnt in years.

After attending my program for two weeks, one of the inmates stopped me and said, "Shiv, I'm going to be released from the prison in a couple of weeks." I asked him what he had learned through the attitude development program. He thought for a while and then said that he felt good about himself. I said, "Good doesn't tell me anything. Tell me specifically what behavior has changed?" (*I believe that learning has not taken place unless behavior changes.*)

He told me that since starting the program, he reads the Bible everyday. I then asked him what reading the Bible did to him. He replied that he now felt comfortable with himself and others, something he hadn't felt before. I said to him, "that is nice, but the bottom line is, what are you going to do when you leave jail?" He told me he was going to try to be a contributing member of society. I asked him the same question again and he gave me the same answer. Then I asked him, "What are you going to do when you leave jail?" Obviously, I was looking for a different answer. At this point, in an angry tone, he said, "I am going to be a contributing member of society." I pointed out to him that there was a world of difference in what he said earlier and what he said now. First he had said, "I am going to try to be" and now he said "I am going to be." The difference is the word "try". Either we do something or we don't. The word "try" keeps the door open for him to come back to jail.

Another inmate, who was listening in on our conversation, asked, "Shiv, what do you get paid to do all this?" I told him, the feeling that I just experienced was worth more than what I could get paid in monetary terms. He then asked, "Why do you come here?" I said, "I come here for my own selfish reasons, I want to make this world a better place to live." This kind of selfishness is healthy. In a nutshell, what you put into the system, you always get back, and most times it is more than you can ever put in. (But you don't put it in with the desire to get something back.)

Another inmate said, "What anybody does is their own business. When people take drugs, it is none of your business.

Why don't you leave them alone?" I replied, "My friend, even though I disapprove, I will compromise and accept what you are saying—that it is none of my business. Can you guarantee that when someone takes drugs, and gets behind the wheel of a car and has an accident, the only thing they will ever hit is a tree, I will compromise. But if you cannot guarantee this, you or I or our kids could be dead, you better believe it is my business. I have to get this person off the roads."

This one phrase, "It is my life, I will do what I want," has done more damage than good. People choose to ignore the spirit and derive the meaning that is convenient to them. Such people have tied this phrase to selfishness and this has had a negative effect on them and the world around them.

These people forget that we don't live in isolation. What you do affects me and what I do affects you. We are connected. We have to realize that we are sharing this planet and we must learn to behave responsibly.

There are two kinds of people in this world—givers and takers. Takers eat well and givers sleep well. Givers have high self-esteem, a positive attitude, and they serve society. By serving society, I do not mean a run-of-the-mill pseudo leader-turned-politician who serves himself by pretending to serve others.

As human beings, we all have the need to receive and take. But a healthy personality with high self-esteem is one that not only has its need to take but also to give.

 A man was washing his new car when his neighbor asked him, "When did you get the car?" He replied "My brother gave it to me." The neighbor said, "I wish I had a car like that." The man replied, "You should wish to have a brother like that." The neighbor's wife was listening to

the conversation and she interrupted, "I wish I was a brother like that." What a positive way to think!

Step 6: Stay Away from Negative Influences

Impressionable minds get influenced by adult behavior and the media. Peer pressure affects not only children and teenagers, it is also prevalent in adults. It shows a lack of self-esteem when people do not have the courage to say "No, thank you," and stay away from negative influences. What are the negative influences?

Negative People

An eagle's egg was placed in the nest of a prairie chicken. The egg hatched and the little eagle grew up thinking it was a prairie chicken. The eagle did what the prairie chickens did. It scratched in the dirt for seeds. It clucked and cackled. It never flew more than a few feet because that is what the prairie chickens did. One day he saw an eagle flying gracefully and majestically in the open sky. He asked the prairie chickens: "What is that beautiful bird?" The chickens replied, "That is an eagle. He is an outstanding bird, but you cannot fly like him because you are just a prairie chicken." So the eagle never gave it a second thought, believing that to be the truth. He lived the life of and died a prairie chicken, depriving himself of his heritage because of his lack of vision. What a waste! He was born to win, but conditioned to lose.

The same thing is true for most people. The unfortunate part of life is as Oliver Wendall Holmes said, "Most people go to their graves, with music still in them." We don't achieve excellence because of our own lack of vision.

If you want to soar like an eagle, you have to learn the ways of an eagle. If you associate with achievers, you will become one. If you associate with thinkers, you will become one. If you associate with givers, you will become one. If you associate with negative people, you will become one.

Whenever people succeed in life, petty people will take cracks at them and try to pull them down. When you refuse to fight petty people, you win. In martial arts, they teach that when someone takes a crack at you, instead of blocking you should step away. Why? Blocking requires energy. Why not use it more productively? Similarly, in order to fight petty people, you have to come down to their level. That is what they want, because now you are one of them.

Don't let negative people drag you down. Remember that a person's character is not only judged by the company they keep but also by the company they avoid.

Smoking, Drugs and Alcohol

One reason that I don't drink is that I want to know when I am having a good time.

— Lady Astor

Drinking makes a person lose his inhibitions and give exhibitions.

In my travels, I have noticed that in some countries drinking has become a national pastime. If you don't drink, they look at you as if there is something wrong. Their motto is: "It doesn't matter how bad your English is, as long as your Scotch is good." If a banker asked them what their liquid assets are, they would bring two bottles of Scotch.

Drinking and smoking are glamorized today. It all starts with the first time. If you ask people why they consume alcohol or take drugs, they will give you a host of reasons, such as: to celebrate; to have fun; to forget problems; to relax; to experiment; to impress others (it is cool to drink); to be fashionable; to mingle; for business purposes.

People want to conform to peer pressure. I am amazed at the way peer pressure compels us with phrases such as "Aren't you my friend?"; "One for the road"; "One for my health."

The following poem from an unknown author explains the dilemma of a social drinker well.

> *I've drunk to your*
> *Health in taverns,*
> *I've drunk to your*
> *Health in my home,*
> *I've drunk to your*
> *Health so damn*
> *many times,*
> *That I've almost*
> *ruined my own!*

Drinking and driving cost lives. Jerry Johnson, in his book *It's Killing Our Kids* (p. xv), cites American Hospital Association reports that half of all hospital admissions are alcohol-related. According to the National Safety Council's 1989 Accident Facts Edition, a person is injured in an alcohol-related crash every 60 seconds.

Pornography

Pornography is nothing short of dehumanizing women and children.

The consequences of pornography are that it

- dehumanizes women
- victimizes children
- destroys marriages
- encourages sexual violence
- makes fun of ethical and moral values
- destroys individuals, families, and communities

A woman is raped in the United States every 46 seconds. (National Victim Center/Crime Victims Research and Treatment Center, 1992). Eighty-six percent of rapists admit to regular use of pornography, with 57 percent admitting imitation of pornography scenes when committing sex crimes (Dr. William Marshall, 1988).*

It is sad to see how low some people will stoop to make a buck by making pornography their business.

Negative Movies and Television Programs

Today's kids are learning their attitudes and values more from television and movies than from any other source. It is estimated that in the United States, by the time a youngster gets out of high school, he has watched more than 20,000 hours of television, witnessed 15,000 murders, and watched 100,000 alcohol-related commercials.** Television programming and advertisements convey the message that drinking is fun, smoking is glamorous, and drugs are the "in" thing. No wonder the crime rate is so high!

---

*From the National Coalition for The Protection of Children and Families, Annual Report, 1995.
**As mentioned in Jerry Johnson's book *It's Killing Our Kids*, p. xvi.

Soap operas and other television shows as well as movies glamorize premarital and extramarital sex. No wonder commitments are lacking in relationships and divorce rates are high. Impressionable viewers set their standards and benchmarks based on what they see and hear in the media. And no matter who we are, we are all impressionable to varying degrees.

Profanity

Using profanities show a lack of vocabulary, self-control, and discipline.

Rock Music

The lyrics of some hit songs are obscene. The music we hear and the performances we watch can subconsciously influence us.

Step 7: Learn to Like the Things That Need to be Done

Start by doing what is necessary, then what is possible, and suddenly you are doing the impossible.
— St. Francis of Assisi

Some things needs to be done whether we like them or not; for example, mothers caring for their young. This may not always be fun, and may even be painful. But if we learn to like the task, the impossible becomes possible.

Step 8: Start Your Day with Something Positive

Read or listen to something positive first thing in the morning. After a good night's sleep we are relaxed and our subconscious is receptive. It sets the tone for the day, and puts us in the right frame of mind to make the day a positive day. In order to bring about change, we need to make a conscious effort and be committed to make positive thoughts and behavior part of our lives. Practice having positive thoughts and behavior daily until they become a habit.

William James of Harvard University said, "*If you are going to change your life, you need to start immediately.*"

If you follow the 8 steps above, you will be a winner:

WINNERS VERSUS LOSERS

- The Winner is always part of the answer;
  The Loser is always part of the problem.
- The Winner always has a program;
  The Loser always has an excuse.
- The Winner says, "Let me do it for you.";
  The Loser says, "That is not my job."
- The Winner sees an answer for every problem;
  The Loser sees a problem for every answer.
- The Winner says, "It may be difficult but it is possible.";
  The Loser says, "It may be possible but it is too difficult."
- When a Winner makes a mistake, he says, "I was wrong.";
  When a Loser makes a mistake, he says, "It wasn't my fault."
- A Winner makes commitments;
  A Loser makes promises.
- Winners have dreams;
  Losers have schemes.
- Winners say, "I must do something.";
  Losers say, "Something must be done."

- Winners are a part of the team;
  Losers are apart from the team.
- Winners see the gain;
  Losers see the pain.
- Winners see possibilities;
  Losers see problems.
- Winners believe in win/win;
  Losers believe for them to win someone has to lose.
- Winners see the potential;
  Losers see the past.
- Winners are like a thermostat;
  Losers are like thermometers.
- Winners choose what they say;
  Losers say what they choose.
- Winners use hard arguments but soft words;
  Losers use soft arguments but hard words.
- Winners stand firm on values but compromise on petty things;
  Losers stand firm on petty things but compromise on values.
- Winners follow the philosophy of empathy: "Don't do to others what you would not want them to do to you";
  Losers follow the philosophy, "Do it to others before they do it to you."
- Winners *make* it happen;
  Losers let it happen.
- Winners plan and prepare to win. The key word is *preparation.*

ACTION STEPS

You may be disappointed if you fail, but you will be doomed if you don't try.

— Beverley Sills

Let me close this chapter with the eight actions steps discussed earlier:

- Look for the positive.
- Make a habit of doing it now.
- Develop an attitude of gratitude.
- Create a continuous education program for yourself.
- Build positive self-esteem.
- Stay away from negative influences.
- Learn to like the things that need to be done.
- Start your day with something positive.

ACTION PLAN

1. Write these action steps down on a 3-by-5 index card and read them every day for the next 21 days.

   For the next 30 minutes, answer the following questions.

2. How can you use each step
   - ➤ at home?
   - ➤ at work?
   - ➤ socially?

3. Make a list of the things you would like to change about yourself.

4. Then list the benefits to you (and others) of each change.

5. Finally establish a time-table—and commit yourself to make the changes.

3

SUCCESS
Winning strategies

Super achievers don't waste time in unproductive thoughts, esoteric thoughts, or catastrophic thoughts. They think constructively and they know that their level of thinking determines their success.

— Dr. Seymour Epstein

YOU need to keep your mind on what you want, not on what you don't want.

Success is not an accident. It is the result of your attitude and your attitude is a choice. Hence success is a matter of choice and not chance.

 A priest was driving when he saw an exceptionally beautiful farm. He stopped at the edge of a field, got out, and stood quietly, appreciating the bountiful crop. The farmer was riding on his tractor and saw the priest. He drove over to where the priest was standing. The priest said to him, "God has blessed you with a beautiful farm. You should be grateful for it." The farmer replied, "Yes, God has blessed me with a beautiful farm and I am grateful for it, but you should have seen this farm when God had the whole farm to himself!"

Most crackpots keep waiting for a jackpot. But that strategy rarely brings success. The common man seeks security, whereas the uncommon man seeks opportunity.

Why does one person move forward with one success story after another, while others are still getting ready?

Why does one man go through life crossing one hurdle after another and accomplishing his goals while another struggles and gets nowhere?

If the answer to these two questions become part of the way you learn, it would revolutionize your life.

WHAT IS SUCCESS?

If you really want to succeed, form the habit of doing things that failures don't like to do.

—Anonymous

A lot of research has been done on the subject of success and failure. The secrets of success can be learnt from the life histories of successful people. Successful people have certain qualities in common no matter which period of history they lived in, and no matter what their fields of endeavor.

Success leaves clues. If we identify and adopt the qualities of successful people, we too shall be successful. Similarly, there are characteristics common to people who aren't successful. If we avoid those characteristics, then we shall not be failures. Success is no mystery. It is simply the result of consistently applying some basic principles. The reverse is just as true: Failure is simply a result of making a few mistakes repeatedly. This might sound too simplistic but the fact is that most truths are very simple. I'm not saying they are easy, but they are simple.

To laugh often and love much;
To win the respect of intelligent persons
and the affection of children;
To earn the approval of honest critics
and endure the betrayal of false friends;
To appreciate beauty;
To find the best in others;
To give of one's self without the
slightest thought of return;
To have accomplished a task, whether
a healthy child, a rescued soul, a

garden patch, or a redeemed social condition;
To have played and laughed with
Enthusiasm and sung with exaltation;
To know that even one life has breathed
easier because you have lived;
This is to have succeeded.

— Anonymous

HOW DO WE DEFINE SUCCESS?

What makes a person successful? How do we recognize success? To some people, success might mean wealth. To others, it is recognition, good health, a good family, happiness, satisfaction, and peace of mind. What this really tells us is that success is subjective. Success means different things to different people. The definition that I feel best summarizes "success" is:

Success is the progressive realization of a worthy goal.

— Earl Nightingale

Let's look at these definitions carefully.

"Progressive" means that success is a journey, not a destination. We never arrive. After we reach one goal, we go on to the next and the next and so on.

"Realization" means it is an experience. Outside forces cannot make me feel successful. I have to feel it within myself. It is internal not external. That is why what often appears as success externally may be total hollowness within.

"Worthiness" refers to our value system without which goals can be unworthy. Which way are we heading? Towards positive or negative goals? Worthiness determines the quality of the journey. That is what gives meaning and fulfillment. Goals are important because they give us a sense of direction.

Success without fulfillment is empty.

I don't know the key to success, but the key to failure is trying to please everybody.

— Bill Cosby

Success does not mean being liked and accepted by everyone. There are some groups I would not, out of choice, want to be accepted by. I would rather be criticized by fools than appreciated by unsavory characters.

I see success as a manifestation of good luck that results from inspiration, aspiration, desperation and perspiration—generally in that sequence.

Success and happiness go hand in hand. Success is getting what you want and happiness is wanting what you get.

Existence alone is not success! It is a lot more!
Do more than exist—live.
Do more than touch—feel.
Do more than look—observe.
Do more than read—absorb.
Do more than hear—listen.
Do more than listen—understand.

— John H. Rhoades

SOME OBSTACLES TO SUCCESS (REAL OR IMAGINED)

- Ego
- Fear of failure/success; lack of self-esteem
- No plan
- Lack of formalized goals
- Life changes
- Procrastination

- Family responsibilities
- Financial security issues
- Lack of focus, being muddled
- Giving up vision for promise of money
- Doing too much alone
- Overcommitment
- Lack of commitment
- Lack of training
- Lack of persistence
- Lack of priorities

THE WINNING EDGE

In order to get the winning edge, we need to strive for excellence, not perfection. Striving for perfection is neurotic; striving for excellence is progress, because there is nothing that can't be done better or improved.

All that we need is a little edge. The winning horse in the race may win with 5-to-1 or 10-to-1 odds. Do you think he is five or ten times faster than the other horses? Of course not. He may only be faster by a fraction, by a nose, but the rewards are five or ten times greater.

Is it fair? Who cares? It doesn't matter. Those are the rules of the game. That is the way the game is played. The same is true in our lives. Successful people are not ten times smarter than the people who fail. They may be fractionally better, but the rewards are ten times bigger.

We don't need to improve 1000% in any one area. All you need is to improve 1% in 1000 different areas, which is a lot easier. That is the winning edge!

STRUGGLE

History has demonstrated that the most notable winners usually encountered heart-breaking obstacles before they triumphed.

They won because they refused to become discouraged by their defeats.

— B.C. Forbes

Trials in life can be tragedies or triumphs, depending on how we handle them. Triumphs don't come without effort.

 A biology teacher was teaching his students how a caterpillar turns into a butterfly. He told the students that in the next couple of hours, the butterfly would struggle to come out of the cocoon, but no one should help the butterfly. Then he left.

The students were waiting and it happened. The butterfly struggled to get out of the cocoon and against the advice of the teacher, one of the students took pity on it and decided to help the butterfly out of the cocoon. He broke the cocoon to help the butterfly so it didn't have to struggle anymore. But, shortly afterwards, the butterfly died.

When the teacher returned, he was told what had happened. He explained to the student that it is a law of nature that the struggle to come out of the cocoon actually helps develop and strengthen the butterfly's wings. By helping the butterfly, the boy had deprived the butterfly of its struggle and the butterfly died.

Apply this same principle to our lives. Nothing worthwhile in life comes without a struggle. As parents we tend to hurt the ones we love most because we don't allow them to struggle to gain strength.

OVERCOMING OBSTACLES

People who have overcome obstacles are more secure than those who have never faced them. We all have problems and sometimes feel discouraged. Everyone faces disappointments; but winners don't get disheartened. The answer is perseverance.

An English proverb says, "A smooth sea never made a skillful mariner." Everything is difficult before it becomes easy. We cannot run away from our problems. Only losers quit and give up.

Most people give up just when they're about to achieve success. They quit on the one-yard line. They give up at the last minute of the game, one foot from a winning touchdown.

— H. Ross Perot

HOW DO WE MEASURE SUCCESS?

True success is measured by the feeling of knowing we have done a job well and have achieved our objective.

Success is not measured by our position in life but by the obstacles we overcame to get there.

Success in life is not determined by *how* we are doing compared with others, but by *how* we are doing compared with what we are capable of doing. Successful people compete against themselves. They better their own record and keep improving constantly.

Success is not measured by how high we go up in life, but rather by how many times we bounce back when we fall down. It is this bounce-back ability that determines success.

EVERY SUCCESS STORY IS ALSO A STORY OF GREAT FAILURE

Failure is the highway to success. Tom Watson Sr., of IBM, said, "If you want to succeed, double your failure rate."

If we study history, we will find that all stories of success are also stories of great failures. But people don't see the failures. They only see the end result and they think that person got lucky: "He must have been at the right place at the right time."

 · Let me share a famous life history with you. This was a man who failed in business at the age of 21; was defeated in a legislative race at age 22; failed again in business at age 24; had his sweetheart die when he was age 26; had a nervous breakdown at age 27; lost a congressional race at age 34; lost a senatorial race at age 45; failed in an effort to become vice-president at age 47; lost a senatorial race at age 49; and was elected president of the United States at age 52. This man was Abraham Lincoln.

Would you call Lincoln a failure? He could have quit, hung his head in shame, and gone back to his law practice. But to Lincoln, defeat was a detour, not a dead end.

 In 1913, Lee De Forest, inventor of the triode tube, was charged by the district attorney for using fraudulent means to mislead the public into buying stocks in his company by claiming that he could transmit the human voice across the Atlantic. He was publicly humiliated. Can you imagine where we would be without his invention?

A New York Times editorial on December 10, 1903 questioned the wisdom of the Wright Brothers who were trying to invent a machine, heavier than air, that would fly. One week later, at Kitty Hawk, the Wright Brothers took their famous flight.

Colonel Sanders, at age 65, had assets of a beat-up car and a $100 check from Social Security. He realized he had to do something to improve his position. He remembered his mother's fried chicken recipe and went out selling. How many doors did he have to knock on before he got his first order? It is estimated that he had knocked on more than a thousand doors before he got his first order. How many of us quit after three tries, ten tries, a hundred tries, and then we say we tried as hard as we could?

As a young cartoonist, Walt Disney faced many rejections from newspaper editors who said he had no talent. One day a minister at a church hired him to draw some cartoons. Disney was working out of a small rodent-infested shed near the church. Seeing a small mouse inspired him to draw a new cartoon. That was the start of Mickey Mouse.

Successful people don't do great things, they only do small things in a great way.

 One day a partially deaf four-year-old child came home with a note in his pocket from his teacher, "Your Tommy is too stupid to learn, get him out of the school." His mother read the note and answered, "My Tommy is not too stupid to learn, I will teach him myself." And that Tommy grew up to be the great Thomas Edison. Thomas Edison had only three months of formal schooling.

Henry Ford forgot to put the reverse gear in the first car he made.

Do you consider these people failures? *They succeeded in spite of problems, not in the absence of them. But to negative thinkers, it appears as though they just "got lucky."*

All success stories are stories of great failures. The only difference is that every time they failed, they bounced back. This is called failing forward, rather than backward. You learn and move forward. Learn from your failure and keep going.

 In 1914, Thomas Edison, at age 67, lost his factory to fire. It had very little insurance. No longer a young man, Edison watched his lifetime effort go up in smoke and said, "There is great value in disaster. All our mistakes are burnt up. Thank God we can start anew." In spite of disaster, three weeks later, he invented the phonograph. What an attitude!

Below are more examples of the failures of successful people:

- Thomas Edison failed approximately 10,000 times while he was working on the light bulb.
- Henry Ford was broke at the age of 40.
- Lee Iacocca was fired by Henry Ford II at the age of 54.
- Young Beethoven was told that he had no talent for music, but he gave some of the best music to the world.

Setbacks are inevitable. A setback can act as a driving force and also teach us humility. In grief, you will find courage and faith to overcome the setback. Learn to become victors, not victims. Fear and doubt short-circuit the mind.

Ask yourself after every setback: What did I learn from this experience? Only then will you be able to turn a stumbling block into a stepping stone.

IF YOU THINK

If you think you are beaten, you are.
If you think you dare not, you don't!
If you like to win, but think you can't,
It's almost a cinch you won't.

If you think you'll lose, you're lost;
For out in the world we find
Success begins with a fellow's will;
It's all in the state of mind.

If you think you are outclassed, you are,
You've got to think high to rise,
You've got to be sure of yourself before
You can ever win a prize.

Life's battles don't always go
To the stronger and faster man,
But sooner or later the man who wins
Is the man who thinks he can.

THE GREATEST GIFT

Of all the creatures in the world, humans are physically the most ill-equipped. A human cannot fly like a bird, outrun a leopard, swim like an alligator, nor climb trees like a monkey. A human doesn't have the eye of an eagle, nor the claws and teeth of a wild cat. Physically, humans are helpless and defenseless; a tiny insect can kill them. But nature is reasonable and kind. Nature's greatest gift to humankind is the ability to think. Humans can create their own environment, whereas animals adapt to their environment.

Sadly, very few people use the greatest gift—the ability to think—to its full potential.

Failures are of two kinds: those who did and never thought and those who thought and never did. Going through life without using your ability to think is like shooting without aiming.

Life is like a cafeteria. You take your tray, select your food and pay at the other end. You can get anything you want as long as you are willing to pay the price. In a cafeteria, if you wait for people to serve you, you will wait forever. Life is like that too. You make choices and pay the price to succeed.

LIFE IS FULL OF CHOICES AND COMPROMISES

Destiny is not a matter of chance, it is a matter of choice; it is not a thing to be waited for, it is a thing to be achieved.

— William Jennings Bryan

At first glance it might seem that there is a contradiction in the statement, that life is full of choices and compromises. If life is full of choices, where is the question of compromise? But, even a compromise is a choice. Let's evaluate this.

How is Life Full of Choices?

When we eat too much, we make a choice to be overweight. When we drink too much, we make a choice to have a headache the next day. If we drink and drive, we choose to risk being killed or killing someone in an accident. When we ill-treat people, we choose to be ill-treated in return. When we don't care about other people, we choose not to be cared for by other people.

Choices have consequences. We are free to make our choice but, after we have chosen, the choice controls us. We have equal opportunity to be unequal. The choice is ours. Life can be compared to a pottery maker who shapes clay in any form he wants. Similarly we can mold our lives into any shape we want.

How is Life Full of Compromises?

Life is not just party and pleasure; it is also pain and despair. Unthinkable things happen. Sometimes everything turns upside down. Bad things happen to good people. Some things are beyond control, such as physical disability and birth defects. We cannot choose our parents or the circumstances of our birth. If the ball bounced the wrong way for you, I'm sorry. But what do you do from that point on—cry or take the ball and run? That is a choice you have to make.

On a clear day, there are hundreds of boats sailing in all different directions in a lake. Even though the wind is blowing in one direction, the sailboats are going in different directions. Why? It depends on the way the sail is set, and that is determined by the sailor. The same is true of our lives. We can't choose the direction of the wind, but we can choose how we set our sail.

Health, happiness, and success depend upon the fighting spirit of each person. The big thing is not what happens to us in life—but what we do about what happens to us.

— George Allen

We can choose our attitude even though we cannot always choose our circumstances. The choice is either to act like a victor or a victim. It is not our position but our disposition that determines our destiny.

It takes both rain and sunshine to create a rainbow. Our lives are no different. There is happiness and sorrow. There is the good and the bad, dark spots and bright spots. When we can handle adversity well, it only strengthens us. We cannot control all the events that happen in our lives, but we can control how we deal with them.

Richard Blechnyden wanted to promote Indian tea at the St. Louis World Fair. It was very hot and no one wanted to sample his tea. Blechnyden saw that iced drinks were doing a flourishing business. It dawned on him to make his tea into an iced drink, mix in some sugar, and offer it for sale. People loved it. That was the introduction of iced tea to the world.* Human beings are not like an acorn which has no choice. An acorn cannot decide whether to become a giant tree or to become food for the squirrels. Human beings have choices. If nature gives us a lemon, we have a choice: either to cry or make lemonade.

When things go wrong, as they sometimes will, you can react responsibly or resentfully—the choice is yours.

QUALITIES THAT MAKE A PERSON SUCCESSFUL

1. Desire

The motivation to succeed comes from the burning desire to achieve a purpose. Napoleon Hill wrote, *"Whatever the mind of man can conceive and believe, the mind can achieve."*

 A young man asked Socrates the secret to success. Socrates told the young man to meet him near the river the next morning. They met. Socrates asked the young man to walk with him toward the river. When the water got up to their necks, Socrates took the young man by surprise and dunked him under the water. The boy struggled to get out but Socrates was strong and held him down. When the boy started turning blue, Socrates raised the boy's head

---

*Adapted from *The Best of .....Bits & Pieces*, Economic Press, Fairfield, NJ, 1994, p. 98.

out of the water. The first thing the young man did was to gasp and take a deep breath of air. Socrates asked, "What did you want the most when you were under water?" The boy replied, "Air." Socrates said, "That is the secret to success. When you want success as intensely as you wanted air underwater, then you will have it." There is no other secret.

A burning desire is the starting point of all accomplishment. Just like a small fire cannot give much heat, a weak desire cannot produce great results.

2. Commitment

Try not to become a success, but rather try to become a man of value.

— Albert Einstein

Integrity and *wisdom* are the two pillars on which to build and keep commitments. This *point is best illustrated by the manager who told one of his staff members, "Integrity is keeping your commitment even if you lose money and wisdom is not to make such foolish commitments."*

Prosperity and success are the result of our thoughts and decisions. It is for us to decide what thoughts will dominate our lives. Success is not an accident. It is the result of our attitude.

Playing to Win Requires Commitment

There is a big difference between playing to win and playing not to lose. When we play to win, we play with enthusiasm and commitment; whereas when we play not to lose, we are playing from a position of weakness. When we play not to lose, we are playing to avoid failure. We all *want* to win, but very few are prepared to pay the price to *prepare* to win. Winners condition and commit themselves to winning. **Playing to win comes out of inspiration, whereas playing not to lose comes out of desperation.**

There are no ideal circumstances. There never will be. To reach any destination, you can neither drift nor lie at anchor. You need to sometimes sail with the wind and sometimes against it, but sail you must.

Ask any coach or athlete to define the difference between the best and the worst team. There would be very little difference in the players' physique, talent and ability. The biggest difference is an emotional difference. The winning team has dedication and they make the extra effort. They have a stronger desire to win. To a winner, the tougher the competition:

- The greater the incentive
- The stronger the motivation
- The better the performance
- The sweeter the victory

New challenges develop new potential. Most athletes' best performances have come when the odds were slightly against them. That is when they dig deeper into their emotional reservoirs.

When I'd get tired and want to stop, I'd wonder what my next opponent was doing. When I could see him still working, I'd start pushing myself. When I could see him in the shower, I'd push myself harder.

— Dan Gable, Olympic gold medallist in wrestling

Success is not in the achievement, but in the achieving. Some people never try because they are afraid to lose. At the same time, they don't want to stay where they are because they are afraid to be left behind. There is a risk either way. Ships that go out into the open waters face risk from a storm. But if they sit in the harbor, they would rust anyway and that is not what they were built for. The difference between playing to win and playing not to lose is that you cannot be committed and not take risks. People who play to win thrive on pressure and those who play not to lose don't know how to succeed.

Pressure makes people who play to win prepare harder. For those who play not to lose, the pressure saps their energy. They want to win, but they are so afraid of losing that they can't reach their full potential. They lose energy worrying about losing instead of concentrating their efforts on winning.

Losers want security; winners seek opportunity. Losers are more afraid of life than death. Failing is not a crime, but lack of effort is.

> *The quality of a person's life is in direct proportion to their commitment to excellence, regardless of their chosen field of endeavor.*
>
> — Vince Lombardi

Conviction Leads to Commitment

There is a difference between preferences and conviction. Preferences are negotiable; convictions are not. Preferences give way under pressure; convictions become stronger. That is why it is important to have a good value system so that our convictions are worthy because convictions in turn lead to commitment.

3. Responsibility

> *A duty which becomes a desire will ultimately become a delight.*
>
> — George Gritter

People with character accept responsibilities. They make decisions and determine their own destiny in life. Accepting responsibilities involves taking risks and being accountable, which is sometimes uncomfortable. Most people would rather stay in their comfort zones and live passive lives without accepting responsibilities. They drift through life waiting for things to happen, rather than making them happen. Accepting responsibilities involves taking calculated, not foolish, risks. It means evaluating all the pros and cons, then taking the most appropriate decision or action. Responsible people don't think that the world owes them a living.

You cannot bring about prosperity by discouraging thrift.
You cannot strengthen the weak by weakening the strong.
You cannot enrich the poor by impoverishing the rich.
You cannot establish sound security on borrowed money.
You cannot help the wage earner by pulling down the wage payer.
You cannot build character and courage by taking away man's initiative and independence.
You cannot further the brotherhood of man by inciting class hatred.
You cannot keep out of trouble by spending more than you earn.
You cannot help men permanently by doing for them what they could and should do for themselves.

— Abraham Lincoln

If you are climbing an icy mountain or fighting a war, a mistake may kill you. However, for most of us, our reactions to the mistakes we make are more important than the mistakes themselves. Responsible people accept and learn from their mistakes. Some people never learn. We can do three things about mistakes:

- Ignore them
- Deny them
- Accept, learn from them and not repeat them.

The third alternative takes courage; it is risky but rewarding. If, instead, we defend our weaknesses, we actually start building our lives around them, making them a centerpoint, rather than overcoming them. **When things go wrong, negative people play the blame game.**

 The retiring president of a company after a standard farewell, gave two envelopes marked No. 1 and No. 2 to the incoming president, and said, "Whenever you run into a management crisis you cannot handle by yourself, open envelope No. 1. At the next crisis, open the second one."

A few years later, a major crisis came. The president went into the safe and pulled out the first envelope. It said, "Blame it on your predecessor." A few years later a second crisis came. The president went for the second envelope, and it said, "Prepare two envelopes for your successor."

4. Hard Work

Luck? I don't know anything about luck. I've never banked on it, and I'm afraid of people who do. Luck to me is something else; hard work—and realizing what is opportunity and what isn't.

—Lucille Ball

Success is not something that you run into by accident. It takes a lot of preparation and character. Everyone likes to win, but most people aren't willing to put in the effort and the time to prepare to win? It takes sacrifice and self-discipline. There is no substitute for hard work. Henry Ford said, "The harder you work, the luckier you get."

The world is full of willing workers, some willing to work and the others willing to let them.

I like to work half a day. I don't care if it is the first 12 hours or the second 12 hours.

—Kammons Wilson, CEO of Holiday Inn

Just as a person cannot learn to spell by sitting on a dictionary or cannot develop a capacity to do anything without hard work. Professionals make things look easy because they have mastered the fundamentals of whatever they do.

If people knew how hard I had to work to gain my mastery, it wouldn't seem wonderful at all.

— Michaelangelo

The average person puts only 25% of his energy and ability into his work. The world takes off its hat to those who put in more than 50% of their capacity, and stands on its head for those few and far between souls who devote 100%.

— Andrew Carnegie

Successful people ask how much work, not how little work; they ask how many hours, not how few. The best musicians practice every day, often for hours. Winners don't need to apologize for winning because they work long and hard.

Everything that we enjoy is a result of someone's hard work. Some work is visible while others go unseen, but ultimately both are equally important. So take pride in your work and whenever there is a chance show appreciation for the hard work of others by treating their work with care and respect. Work hard and well and you will have the satisfaction of seeing your project completed. Sometimes others may show appreciation, but that's a bonus: For the major satisfaction comes from within.

Some people stop working as soon as they find a job. Regardless of the unemployment statistics, it is hard to find good people to work.

Many people don't understand the difference between idle time and leisure time. Idle time amounts to wasting or stealing time; leisure time is earned. Enjoying leisure time leaves us energized and refreshed. Idle time saps our energy. Procrastinating is idle time.

Excellence is not luck; it is the result of a lot of hard work and practice. Hard work and practice make a person better at whatever he is doing.

Far and away the best prize that life offers is the chance to work hard at something worth doing.

— Theodore Roosevelt

Hard work is both a beginning and an end in itself. The harder a person works, the better he feels; and the better he feels, the harder he works. The best ideas will not work unless you work the ideas. Great talent without will-power and hard work is a waste.

We need to learn from nature. The duck keeps paddling relentlessly underneath but appears smooth and calm on the top.

Once when the great violinist Fritz Kreisler finished a concert, someone came up to the stage and said, "I'd give my life to play the way you do." Kreisler replied, "I did!"

There is no magic wand for success. In the real world, success comes to doers, not observers. A horse that pulls cannot kick; a horse that kicks cannot pull. Let's pull and stop kicking.

Without hard work there is no success.

Nature gives birds their food but does not put it in their nests. They have to work hard for it. Nothing comes easily. Milton rose every morning at 4 a.m. to write *Paradise Lost*. It took Noah Webster 36 years to compile *Webster's Dictionary*.

Even small accomplishments require hard work. The smallest of accomplishments is better than the biggest talk.

5. Character

Character is the sum total of a person's values, beliefs and personality. It is reflected in our behavior and in your actions. It needs to be preserved more than the richest jewel in the world. To be a winner takes character. George Washington said, " I hope I shall always possess firmness and virtue enough to maintain what I consider the most valuable of all titles, the character of an honest man."

It is not the polls or public opinion but the character of the leader that determines the course of history. There is no twilight zone in integrity. The road to success has many pitfalls. It takes a lot of character and effort not to fall into them. It also takes character not to be disheartened by critics.

Why do most people love success but hate successful people? Whenever a person rises above the average, plenty of people are ready to pull him down. Chances are pretty good when you see a person on top of a hill, that he just didn't get there by default, but had to endure a tough climb. It's no different in life. In any profession, a successful person will be envied by those who are not successful. Critics have always been sitting at the sidelines. They are underachievers who shout at doers, telling them how to do it right. But remember, critics are not the leaders or doers. Don't let criticism distract you from reaching your goal. Average people play it safe to avoid criticism. By saying, doing or being nothing, they avoid criticism and guarantee that they remain average. The more you accomplish, the more you risk being criticized.

The critic is one who knows the price of everything and the value of nothing.

— Oscar Wilde

No one likes to be criticized, but we learn and grow from honest criticism. Just as it takes character not to be disheartened by critics, it also takes character to listen to critics. It is very important to be able to distinguish honest criticism from jealousy-inspired criticism, this is a skill that successful people have. Part of this skill is being able to evaluate the motive of the criticizer. The other part, and perhaps the largest part, is self-knowledge. The successful person knows himself well enough to recognize when a particular criticism is valid.

Successful people don't like to be criticized any more than anyone else does. But when they deem the criticism valid, they remain calm and in control and listen carefully. They ask for suggestions on how to improve. In fact, successful people often ask for criticism from those whose opinions they trust. They ask: "How am I doing?" "How can I improve?"

Character is a Combination

Character is a combination of integrity, unselfishness, understanding, conviction, courage, loyalty and respect.
What is a pleasant personality with character?

- It is in a class by itself.
- It is composure.
- It is poise.
- It is surefootedness and confidence without arrogance.
- It is being considerate.
- It is never making excuses.
- It is knowing that courtesy and good manners take many small sacrifices.
- It is learning from past mistakes.
- It has nothing to do with money or blue blood.
- It never builds itself by destroying others.
- It is substance, not just form.
- It is being able to walk with the elite and yet maintain the common touch.
- It is a gentle word, a kind look and a good-natured smile.
- It is the secret pride that stands against tyranny.
- It is being comfortable with oneself and others.
- It is having the classic touch that gives the winning edge.
- It works wonders.
- It accomplishes miracles.
- It is easy to recognize, hard to define.
- It is accepting responsibility.
- It is humility.
- It is graciousness in victory and defeat.
- It is not fame and fortune.

- It is not a plaque.
- It is permanent.
- It is intangible.
- It is being courteous and polite without being subservient.
- It is being classy without being cocky.
- It is self-discipline and knowledge.
- It is self-contained.
- It is a gracious winner and an understanding loser.

Something in human nature causes us to start slacking off at our moment of greatest accomplishment. As you become successful, you will need a great deal of self-discipline not to lose your sense of balance, humility and commitment.

— H. Ross Perot

More difficult than success itself is how we handle success. Many people know how to become successful, but after they become successful they don't know how to handle it. That is why ability and character go hand in hand. Ability will get you success; character will keep you successful.

We don't unfold or discover ourselves—we create and build ourselves into the kind of person we want to be.

Character-building starts from infancy and goes on until death. Character does not need success. It is success. Just like a gardener has to keep weeding to prevent weeds from eating the life of the garden, we need to keep building and developing our character by weeding out our faults.

Adversity Builds and/or Reveals Character

Under adverse circumstances, some people break records and others break down. John F. Kennedy once said that it is a mark of character how well a person behaves when things are not going well. When things are going well for us, it is easy to be logical, kind and gracious. But when things aren't going well and we're under a lot of pressure, some people can't think clearly and snap at others around them, while others remain clear-headed and continue to treat others with respect. Adversity reveals a person's character.

There is a Russian saying: "A hammer shatters glass but forges steel." There is a lot of truth in the saying. Are we made of glass or steel? It is the same hammer.

Just as carbon determines the quality of steel, character determines the quality of a man.

6. Positive Believing

What is the difference between positive thinking and positive believing? What if you could actually listen to your thoughts? Are they positive or negative? Are you programming your mind for success or failure? The way in which you think has a profound effect on your performance.

Having a positive attitude and being motivated is a choice we make every day. Living a positive life is not easy; but then neither is negative living. Given a choice, I would rather go for a positive living. Positive thinking helps you use your abilities to the fullest.

Positive believing is more than positive thinking. It is knowing that positive thinking will work. Positive believing is an attitude of confidence that comes from preparation.

Having a positive attitude without making the effort is nothing more than having a wishful dream. The following illustrates positive believing.

 Several years ago Lockheed introduced the L-1011 Tristar plane. In order to ensure safety and test the strength of the jetliner, Lockheed exposed the plane to the roughest possible treatment for 18 months, a program that cost $1.5 billion. Hydraulic jacks, electronic sensors, and a computer put the airplane through its paces for more than 36,000 simulated flights (equivalent to 100 years of airline service), without one single malfunction. Finally after thousands of tests, the aircraft was given the seal of approval.*

Does the Lockheed organization have reason to believe positively? You bet. There is every reason to believe that this plane is safe to fly, because of all the effort put into preparation.

7. Give More Than You Get

It is easy to succeed today. If you want to get ahead in life, go the extra mile. There is no competition on the extra mile. Are you willing to do a little more than you get paid for? How many people you know are willing to do a little bit more than what they get paid for? Hardly any.

Most people don't want to do what they get paid for and a second category of people want only to do what

*Adapted from *Daily Motivations for African-American Success* by Dennis Kimbro, June 29, 1993, Fawcett Press, New York.

they can get by with. They fulfill their quotas just to keep their jobs. Only a small fraction is willing to do a little bit more than what they get paid for. Why do they do more?

The advantages of doing more than you get paid for are:

- You make yourself more valuable, regardless of what you do and where you work.
- It gives you more confidence.
- People start looking at you as a leader.
- Others start trusting you.
- Superiors start respecting you.
- It breeds loyalty from both your subordinates and your superiors.
- It generates cooperation.
- It produces pride and satisfaction.

If we go the extra mile, where is the competition?

If you work for a man, for heaven's sake work for him.

— Kim Hubbard

Hard working people are in demand everywhere regardless of age, experience or academic qualifications. Hard-working people:

- Can work without supervision.
- Are punctual and considerate.
- Listen carefully and carry out instructions accurately.
- Tell the truth.
- Don't sulk when called upon to pitch in at the time of an emergency.
- Are result oriented rather than task oriented.
- Are cheerful and courteous.

Always think in terms of giving more than is expected by your customer, friends, spouse, parents and children. Whenever you do anything, ask yourself, "How can I add value to what I am doing?" or "How can I give added value to others?"

The key to success can be summed up in four words: "and then some more." Winners do what they are supposed to—and then some more. Winners do their duty—and then some more. Winners are courteous and generous—and then some more. Winners can be counted on—and then some more. Winners put in 100%—and then some more.

Ability without dependability, responsibility and flexibility is a liability.

Why are some highly intelligent people, often with impressive academic qualifications, living failures or at best, practicing mediocrity? Because they become experts at why things won't work and build a reserve of negative energy. They don't want to do what they get paid for or they only want to do what they can get by with. No wonder they are living failures. When we give or do more than what we get paid for, we eliminate our competition. In fact, we become the competition. This attitude is much more important than intelligence or a degree.

8. The Power of Persistence

Nothing will take the place of persistence. Talent will not: Nothing is more common than unsuccessful people with talent. Genius will not: Unrewarded genius is a proverb. Education will not: The world is full of educated derelicts. Persistence and determination alone are omnipotent.

— Calvin Coolidge

The journey to being your best is not easy. It is full of setbacks. Winners have the ability to overcome and bounce back with even greater resolve.

DON'T QUIT

When things go wrong,
As they sometimes will,
When the road you're trudging seems all uphill,
When the funds are low and the debts are high,
And you want to smile, but you have to sigh,
When care is pressing you down a bit—
Rest if you must, but don't you quit.

Life is queer with its twists and turns,
As every one of us sometimes learns,
And many a failure turns about
When he might have won had he stuck it out.
Don't give up though the pace seems slow—
You may succeed with another blow.

Success is failure turned inside out—
The silver tint of the clouds of doubt,
And you never can tell how close you are,
It may be near when it seems so far;
So stick to the fight when you're hardest hit
It's when things seem worst that you mustn't quit.

 Fritz Kreisler, the great violinist, was once asked, "How do you play so well? Are you lucky?" He replied, "It is practice. If I don't practice for a month, the audience can tell the difference. If I don't practice for a week, my wife can tell the difference. If I don't practice for a day, I can tell the difference."

Persistence results from commitment and leads to determination. There is pleasure in endurance. Athletes put in years of practice for a few seconds or minutes of performance.

Persistence is a decision. It is a commitment to finish what you start. When we are exhausted, quitting looks good. But winners endure. Ask a winning athlete. He endures pain and finishes what he started. Lots of people who are failures began well but never finished anything. Persistence comes from purpose. Life without purpose is drifting. A person who has no purpose will never persevere and will never be fulfilled.

9. Pride of Performance

In today's world, pride in performance has fallen by the wayside because it requires effort and hard work. However, nothing happens unless it is made to happen. When one is discouraged, it is easy to look for shortcuts. However these should be avoided no matter how great the temptation. Pride comes from within—it is what gives the winning edge.

Pride of performance does not represent ego. It represents pleasure with humility. *The quality of the work and the quality of the worker are inseparable.* Half-hearted effort does not produce half results; it produces no results.

 Three people were laying bricks. A passerby asked them what they were doing. The first one replied, "Don't you see I am making a living?" The second one said, "Don't you see I am laying bricks?" The third one said, "I am building a beautiful monument." Here were three people doing the same thing who had totally different perspectives on what

they were doing. They had three very different attitudes about their work. And would their attitude affect their performance? The answer is clearly yes.

Excellence comes when the performer takes pride in doing his best. Every job is a self-portrait of the person who does it, regardless of what the job is, whether washing cars, sweeping the floor or painting a house.

Do it right the first time, every time. The best insurance for tomorrow is a job well done today.

Michelangelo had been working on a statue for many days. He was taking a long time to retouch every small detail. A bystander thought these improvements were insignificant, and asked Michelangelo why he bothered with them. Michelangelo replied, "Trifles make perfection and perfection is no trifle."

Most people forget how fast you did a job, but they remember how well it was done.

> *If a man is called to be streetsweeper, he should sweep streets even as Michelangelo painted, or Beethoven composed music, or Shakespeare wrote poetry. He should sweep streets so well that all the hosts of heaven and earth will pause to say, here lived a great streetsweeper who did his job well.*

> — Martin Luther King, Jr.

The feeling of a job well done is a reward in itself. It is better to do small things well than do many things poorly.

10. Be a Willing to Be a Student—Get a Mentor

If God and the teacher (guru) are standing together, who does the student salute first? According to Indian culture, the answer is the teacher, because without his direction and help, the student could not have met God.

A mentor or a teacher is a person whose hindsight can become your foresight. Look for someone who can mentor you. Choose your mentor carefully. A good mentor will guide and give direction, whereas a bad mentor will misguide. Show respect. Be an interested student. An interested student gets the best out of a teacher.

The best teachers will not give you something to drink, they will make you thirsty. They will put you on a path to seek answers.

DO YOU HAVE WHAT IT TAKES TO BE SUCCESSFUL?

Do all of us have the qualities for success? Some people feel they don't. They stay mediocre and fail. But it doesn't have to be that way. All of us possess each of the ten qualities discussed in this chapter. The qualities may not be developed to the level that you want them to be, but they are there. We may not know that they are there, but when we find out, our performance will change.

This is like having a million dollars buried in your backyard and not knowing about it. You wouldn't be able to use it. But the moment you find out, your thinking and behavior will change. We all have hidden treasures. All we need to do is bring them to the surface and use them.

ACTION PLAN

Success seems to be connected with action. Successful people keep moving. They make mistakes, but they don't quit.

— Conrad Hilton

1. To achieve success, you must have a worthwhile goal. Write down your most important goals.

   _____

   _____

   _____

2. To achieve success, you must overcome failure. What failures have you overcome so far?

   _____

   _____

   _____

3. Ben Franklin identified 13 virtues and worked on each of them for a week. At the end of 13 weeks, he started the cycle over again. Decide how you can work on each of the ten keys to success in this chapter.

- Desire

- Commitment

- Responsibility

- Hard work

- Character

- Positive believing

- Give more than you get

- Persistence

- Pride of performance

- Be a student; get a mentor

4

WHAT IS HOLDING US BACK?

The only limit to our realization of tomorrow will be our doubts of today.

— Franklin D. Roosevelt

WHAT would happen if you drove your car with the brakes on? You'd never go full speed because the brakes would offer resistance. Your car would overheat and break down. If it didn't break down, the resistance would strain the engine. To get to your destination, you would have to make one of two choices: You could either press the accelerator harder and risk damage, or release the brakes to make the car go faster.

This analogy is a good parallel to life because many of us go through life with our emotional brakes on. What are the brakes? They are the factors that prevent you from achieving success—fear, procrastination, lack of pride and so forth. The way to release your emotional brakes is by building a positive attitude and high self-esteem and by accepting responsibility.

FAILURE—20 REASONS WHY WE DON'T ACHIEVE EXCELLENCE

Life is like a ten-speed bicycle. Most of us have gears we never use.

— Charles Schultz

There are 20 factors that can cause you to fail. By working to overcome these factors, you can release the brakes that are holding back your success.

1. Unwillingness to Take Risks

Success involves taking calculated risks. Risk-taking does not mean gambling foolishly and behaving irresponsibly. People sometimes mistake irresponsible and rash behavior as risk-taking. They end up with negative results and blame it on bad luck.

Risk-taking is relative. The concept of risk varies from person to person and can be a result of training. To both a trained mountain climber and a novice, mountain climbing is risky, but to the trained person it is not irresponsible risk-taking. Responsible risk-taking is based on knowledge, training, careful study, confidence and competence—factors that give you the courage to act while facing fear. The person who never attempts anything risky makes no mistakes. However, not making the attempt is often a bigger mistake than making the attempt and failing.

Indecision is habit forming and contagious. Many opportunities are lost because of indecision. Take risks, but don't gamble. Risk-takers move ahead with their eyes open. Gamblers shoot in the dark.

 Once someone asked a farmer if he had planted wheat for the season. The farmer replied, "No. I was afraid it wouldn't rain." The man asked, "Did you plant corn?" The farmer said, "No. I was afraid that insects would eat the corn." Then the man asked, "What did you plant?" The farmer said, "Nothing. I played it safe."

RISKS

To laugh is to risk appearing the fool.
To weep is to risk appearing sentimental.
To reach out for another is to risk involvement.
To expose feelings is to risk exposing your true self.
To place your ideas, your dreams, before a crowd is to risk their loss.
To love is to risk not being loved in return.

To live is to risk dying.
To hope is to risk despair.
To try is to risk failure.

But risks must be taken, because the greatest
hazard in life is to risk nothing.
The person who risks nothing, does nothing, has
nothing, and is nothing.
They may avoid suffering and sorrow, but they
cannot learn, feel, change, grow, love, or live.
Chained by their attitudes, they are slaves,
they have forfeited their freedom.
Only a person who risks is free.

2. Lack of Persistence

When problems seem insurmountable, quitting may
look like the easiest way out. It is true for every marriage,
job and relationship. Winners are struck but not destroyed. We all have had our setbacks in life. But failing
does not mean we are failures.

What is the difference between *persistence* and *obstinacy*?
The difference is that persistence represents a strong will
and obstinacy represents a strong won't!

Most people fail not because they lack knowledge or
talent but because they quit. The total secret of success
lies in two traits: persistence and resistance. *Persist*
in what must be done and *resist* from what ought not to
be done.

A man is a hero not because he is braver than anyone else,
but because he is brave for ten minutes longer.

— Ralph Waldo Emerson

3. Instant Gratification

The desire to make a million overnight has made the lottery a flourishing business. We are living in an age of instant gratification. There is a pill for everything, from waking you up to putting you to sleep. People want to take a pill to get rid of their problems. In the same way when people want to be instant millionaires, they take shortcuts and compromise on their integrity.

Remember that when going for instant gratification, one never thinks of consequences, only of momentary pleasures.

Today's generation defines the ideal diet as one that will take off five pounds for good intentions. These are people who don't want any more birthdays but want all the presents.

When you think short term, not long term, it is limited vision. With limited vision you will never see any worthwhile goals.

4. Lack of Priorities

People make substitutions where they ought not to. For example, in relationships, they trade money and gifts for affection and time. Some people find it easier to buy things for their children and spouse to compensate for their absence than to spend time interacting with them.

When we don't have our priorities right, we waste time, not realizing that time wasted is life wasted. Prioritizing requires discipline to do what needs to be done rather than taking action based on our moods and fancies. These days too much emphasis is placed on success and failure rather than doing one's best.

How do you cope with defeat and problems?

Your response to this question says a lot about your character. One of the keys to solving this mystery of success is understanding your priorities. Some people set their sights on money, power, fame or possessions. We have to understand our priorities.

Success does not come by reading or memorizing the principles that lead to success, but by understanding them and setting your priorities to apply them.

5. Looking for Shortcuts

No Free Lunch

A king called his advisers and asked them to write down the wisdom of the ages so that he could pass it on to future generations. After a lot of work, the advisers came up with several volumes of wisdom and presented them to the king. The king called his advisers and said that it was too long and that people would not read it. The king told his advisers they would have to condense it. The advisers went back to work and came back with one volume. The king said it was still too long so they came back again with one chapter; again it was too long. Even one page was too long, said the king. Finally, the advisers brought back one sentence that satisfied the king. He said that if there was one piece of wisdom that he wanted to pass on to future generations, it would be: "There is no free lunch."

Basically, "there is no free lunch," means that you don't get something for nothing. In other words, you get what you put in. If you don't put much into a project, you won't get much out of it.

Of course every society has its share of free loaders who are looking for something for nothing.

The Easier Way May Actually Be the Tougher Way

Once there was a lark singing in the forest. A farmer came by with a box full of worms. The lark stopped him and asked, "What do you have in the box and where are you going?" The farmer replied that he had worms and that he was going to the market to trade them for some feathers. The lark said, "I have many feathers. I will pluck one and give it to you and that will save me looking for worms." The farmer gave the worms to the lark and the lark plucked a feather and gave it in return. The next day the same thing happened and the day after and on and on until a day came that the lark had no more feathers. Now it could no longer fly to go hunting for worms. It started looking ugly and stopped singing and very soon it died.

The moral of this story is quite clear—what the lark thought was an easy way to get food turned out to be the tougher way after all.

Isn't the same thing true in our lives? Many times we look for the easier way, which really ends up being the tougher way.

Losers Look for Quick Fixes

There are two ways of getting rid of weeds in your yard: the easy way and the not-so-easy way. The easy way may be to run a lawnmower; the yard looks fine for a while, but it is only a temporary solution. Soon the weeds are back. The not-so-easy way means getting down on your hands and knees and pulling out the weeds by the roots. It is time-consuming and painful, but the weeds will stay away for a longer time. The first solution appeared easy, but the problem remained. The second solution was not so easy, but took care of the problem from the roots. The key is to get to the root of the problem. The same is true of our attitudes in life. Some people spread their attitudes of bitterness and resentment and these attitudes keep cropping up in different parts of their lives.

The problem with people today is that they want instant answers. They are looking for one-minute solutions to everything. Like instant coffee they want instant happiness, but there are no quick fixes. This attitude leads to disappointment.

6. Selfishness and Greed

Individuals and organizations that have a selfish attitude have no right to expect growth. Their attitude is to keep passing the buck without regard for the welfare of others. Greed always wants more. Needs can be satisfied, but greed cannot. It is a cancer of the soul. Greed destroys relationships.

Greed comes out of poor self-esteem, which manifests itself as false pride, pretence, or "keeping up with the Joneses." The way out of greed is to learn to live within your means and be satisfied. Being content does not mean lack of ambition.

 **WHERE DOES IT END?**

A wealthy farmer was once offered all the land he could walk on in a day provided he returned by sundown to the point at which he started. To get a head start, early the next morning, the farmer started covering ground quickly because he wanted to get as much land as he could. Even though he was tired, he kept going all afternoon because he didn't want to lose this once-in-a-lifetime opportunity to gain more wealth.

Late in the afternoon, he remembered that the condition he had to fulfil to get the land was to get back to the starting point by sundown. His greed had gotten him far from the starting point. He started his return journey, keeping an eye on how close he was to sundown. The closer it got to sundown, the faster he ran. He was exhausted and out of breath, and he pushed himself beyond the point of endurance. He collapsed upon reaching the starting point and died. He did make it before sundown. He was buried and all the land he needed was a small plot.

There is a lot of truth in this story and a lesson to be learned. Whether the farmer was wealthy or not, any greedy person would have ended the same way.

7. Lack of Conviction

People who lack conviction take the middle of the road. And, guess what happens to those in the middle of the road. They get run over!

People without conviction do not take a stand. They go along to get along because they lack confidence and courage. They conform in order to get accepted even when they know that what they are doing is wrong.

Some people consider themselves a shade better because they do not support the wrong; however, they lack the conviction to oppose. But by not opposing something you know is wrong, you are actually supporting it.

One of the important secrets to success is, instead of being against something, be *for* something. That way, you don't become part of the problem, but part of the solution. It takes conviction to take a stand.

Conviction Takes Faith

Faith without action is delusion. Faith does not wait for miracles but produces them.

If you think you can or if you think you can't, you are right.

— Henry Ford

We all have low moments; we all fall down and get hurt. We all have moments when we doubt ourselves and indulge in self-pity. The point is to overcome these feelings and restore your faith.

There are three kinds of people in this world:

1. People who make things happen
2. People who watch things happen
3. People who wonder what happened

Which category do you fall into?

8. Lack of Understanding of Nature's Laws

How many times it thundered before Franklin took the hint! How many apples fell on Newton's head before he took the hint! Nature is always hinting at us. It hints over and over again. And suddenly we take the hint.

— Robert Frost

Success is a matter of laws and we are referring to the laws of nature. Change is nature's law. We are either moving forward or we are going backward. We are either creating or disintegrating. There is no status quo.

A seed, if it is not planted in the earth to create, disintegrates. Change is inevitable. It is going to happen whether you like it or not. *All progress is change but all change is not progress.* We must evaluate change and accept it only if it makes sense. Acceptance without evaluation amounts to conforming behavior, a sign of lack of confidence and low self-esteem.

There is a lot to be said about tradition. Growth for the sake of growth is the philosophy of a cancerous cell. It is negativity spreading all over. That is not growth, that is destruction. Growth, in order to be meaningful, must be positive.

Success is not a matter of luck, but of laws.

Law of Cause and Effect

In order to succeed, we need to understand the law of cause and effect and the relationship between actions and results.

For every effect, there is a cause. The law of cause and effect is the same as the law of sowing and reaping. The laws of sowing and reaping are:

1. You must have the desire to sow. Desire is the starting point.
2. What you sow, so shall you reap. If you sow potatoes, you are only going to reap potatoes, not tomatoes.
3. You must sow before you reap. Sowing takes place before reaping; you must give before you get. You cannot expect the fireplace to give heat before you put in the fuel. Some people are constantly looking to get before they give. It does not work this way.
4. When you sow a seed, you reap manifold. If you sow a positive seed, your harvest will be manifold in the positive and, if you sow a negative seed your harvest will be manifold in the negative. It is not uncommon to see people going against nature's law.
5. A farmer knows that you cannot sow and reap in the same day. There is always a period of gestation.
6. You sow sparingly, you reap sparingly. You sow abundantly, you reap abundantly.

It is like the law of physics. For every action, there is an equal and opposite reaction. Most of the time people are trying to change the effect while the cause remains. Either you constantly feed your mind with positives or negativity automatically fills the vacuum. Many ancient sages have also said what James Allen said in his book *As a Man Thinketh.* A man's mind is like a garden. If we plant good seeds, we will have a good garden. But if we don't plant anything, something will grow and that will be weeds. That is nature's law.

The same holds true in our lives. In fact I would go a step further. Even if we plant good seeds, weeds would still grow. The process of weeding goes on forever.

If you put water in a glass and put it in sub-zero temperature, it will freeze. That is not surprising. This is nature's law. In fact, that is the only thing that will happen.

Our thoughts are causes.

You sow a thought, you reap an action.
You sow an action, you reap a habit.
You sow a habit, you reap a character.
You sow a character, you reap a destiny.
It all starts with a thought.

Laws of Attraction

We attract to ourselves not what we want but what we are. The old phrase, "Birds of a feather flock together," holds true.

Negative thinkers are dangerous. They attract other negative people, react negatively and expect the worst and they are not disappointed.

Have you observed how at any social occasion successful people attract other successful people? Failures attract other failures, and together they will moan, groan and complain.

Our friends are not the kind of people we want but the kind of people we are.

9. Unwillingness to Plan and Prepare

Everyone has a will to win but very few have the will to prepare to win.

— Vince Lombardi

Most people spend more time planning a party or vacation than planning their lives.

Preparation

Confidence comes from preparation, which is nothing but planning and practicing. Winners put pressure on themselves. That is the pressure of preparing and not worrying about winning.

If we practice poorly, we play poorly; because we play as we practice. The difference between success and failure is the difference between doing exactly right and almost right.

A complete mental and physical preparation is the result of sacrifice and self-discipline. It is easy to be average but tough to be the best. No wonder the average people choose the easy way.

Preparation is the necessary edge to succeed in any field.

Preparation = Purpose + Principle + Planning + Practice + Perseverance + Patience + Pride

Preparation Leads to Confidence

Preparation means tolerating failure but never accepting it. It means having the courage to face defeat without feeling defeated, being disappointed without being discouraged.

Preparation means learning from our mistakes. There is nothing wrong with making mistakes. We all do. A fool is one who makes the same mistake twice. A person who makes a mistake and doesn't correct it, commits a bigger one.

The best way to handle a mistake is to:

- Admit to it quickly
- Not dwell on it
- Learn from it
- Never repeat it
- Not assign blame or make excuses.

Pressure comes from being unprepared. There is no substitute for preparation, practice and hard work. Desire and wishful thinking won't do it. Only preparation will give you the competitive edge.

Pressure can paralyze you if you are not prepared. Just as water gravitates to its own path, success gravitates to those who are prepared. Weak effort gets weak results.

Persistence is a name we give to:

- a purpose
- preparation
- patience
- principles
- positive attitude
- a plan
- pride
- practice
- price

Ask yourself:

- Do you have a clearly defined purpose?
- Do you have a plan of action?
- What effort are you putting into preparation?
- What price are you willing to pay? How far are you willing to go?
- Do you have the patience to withstand the gestation period?
- Are you willing to practice toward excellence?
- Do you have any firm principles to stand on?
- Do you have pride in your performance?
- Do you have the "can do " attitude?

10. Rationalizing

Winners may analyze but they never rationalize—that is a loser's game. Losers always have a book full of excuses to tell you why they could not. We hear excuses like:

- I'm unlucky.
- I'm born under the wrong stars.
- I'm too young.
- I'm too old.
- I'm handicapped.
- I'm not smart enough.
- I'm not educated.
- I'm not good looking.
- I don't have contacts.
- I don't have enough money.
- I don't have enough time.
- The economy is bad.
- If only I had the opportunity.
- If only I didn't have a family.
- If only I had married right.

The list can go on and on. There are two things that

determine whether a person will be a success: reasons and results. Reasons don't count while results do.

How They Catch Monkeys in India

Monkey-hunters use a box with an opening at the top, big enough for the monkey to slide its hand into. Inside the box are nuts. The monkey grabs the nuts and now its hand becomes a fist. The monkey tries to get its hand out but the opening is big enough for the hand to slide into, but too small for the fist to come out of. Now the monkey has a choice, either to let go off the nuts and be free forever or hang on to the nuts and get caught. Guess what it picks every time? You guessed it. He hangs on to the nuts and gets caught.

We are no different from monkeys. We all hang on to the nuts that keep us from going forward in life. We keep rationalizing by saying, "I cannot do this because ..." and whatever comes after "because" are the nuts that we are hanging onto that are holding us back.

Successful people don't rationalize. Good advice for failure is: Don't think, don't ask, and don't listen. Just rationalize.

11. Not Learning from Past Mistakes

While one person hesitates because he feels inferior, the other is busy making mistakes and becoming superior.

— Henry C. Link

People who do not learn lessons from history are doomed. We learn from failure if we have the right attitude. Failure is a detour, not a dead end. It is a delay, not a defeat. Experience is the name we give to our mistakes.

Some people live and learn, and some only live. Wise

people learn from their mistakes—wiser people learn from other people's mistakes. Our lives are not long enough to learn only from our own mistakes!

12. Inability to Recognize Opportunity

Opportunities can come disguised as obstacles. That is why most people don't recognize them. Remember, the bigger the obstacle, the better is the opportunity.

13. Fear

Fear can be real or imaginary. Fear makes people do strange things. It primarily comes from a lack of understanding. To live in fear is to live in an emotional prison.

Fear results in insecurity, lack of confidence and procrastination. It destroys our potential and ability. We cannot think straight. Fear ruins relationships and health.

Some common fears are:

- Fear of failing
- Fear of the unknown
- Fear of being unprepared
- Fear of making the wrong decision
- Fear of rejection

Some fears can be described, others can only be felt. Fear leads to anxiety which in turn leads to irrational thinking. And this actually sabotages our ability to solve problems. The normal response to fear is escape. Escape puts us in a comfort zone and reduces the impact of fear temporarily, while the cause remains. Imaginary fears magnify the problem. Fear can get out of hand and destroy happiness and relationships. Think of fear as meaning:

F	E	A	R
A	V	P	E
L	I	P	A
S	D	E	L
E	E	A	
	N	R	
	C	I	
	E	N	
		G	

Fear of failure is often worse than failure itself. Failure is not the worst thing that can happen to someone. People who don't try have failed even before attempting. When infants learn to walk, they keep falling; but to them it is not failing, it is learning. If they became disheartened, they would never walk. It is better to die on one's feet than to live with fear on one's knees.

14. Inability to Use Talent

Albert Einstein said, "I think I used about 25% of my intellectual capacity during my life."

According to William James, human beings use only 10–12% of their potential.*

The saddest part of most people's lives is that they die with the music still in them.

They haven't lived life while alive. They rust out rather than wear out. I would rather wear out than rust out. The saddest words in life are: "I should have."

Rusting out is not to be confused with patience. Patience is a conscious decision, it is active and involves

---

* William James, *MDRT Timeless Treasure*, The Whole Person, p. 162.

perseverance and persistence. Rusting out is idleness and passivity.

Someone asked an elderly person, "What is life's heaviest burden?" The elderly person replied sadly, "To have nothing to carry."

15. Lack of Discipline

You have a choice in life: You can either pay the price of discipline or regret.

—Tim Connor

Have you ever wondered why some people never reach their goals? Why they are always frustrated with reversals and crises? Why do some people have continued success, while others have endless failures? Anyone who has accomplished anything worthwhile has never done so without discipline, whether in sports, athletics, academia or business.

People without discipline try to do everything, but commit themselves to nothing. Some so-called liberal thinkers have interpreted lack of discipline as freedom. When I am in an aircraft I want a pilot who is disciplined and does what he is supposed to do and not what he feels like doing. I don't want him to have the philosophy, "I'm free. I don't want anyone from the control tower telling me what to do."

Lack of consistency is poor discipline. Discipline takes self-control, sacrifice, and avoiding distractions and temptations. It means staying focused. Steam does not move the engine unless it is confined. Niagara Falls would not generate power unless it were harnessed.

We all know the story of the tortoise and the hare. The hare bragged about his speed and challenged the tortoise to a race. The tortoise accepted the challenge. They appointed a fox as the judge. The race started and the tortoise kept going, slowly but the hare sprinted off. He quickly left the tortoise behind. As he was confident of winning the race he decided to take a nap. By the time he woke up, remembered the race, and resumed running, the tortoise had already reached the finish line and won.

Consistency takes discipline and is more important than erratic effort.

Discipline and regret are both painful. Most people have a choice between the two. Guess which is more painful.

Generally children brought up with excessive freedom and a lack of discipline grow up not respecting themselves, their parents or society, and have a hard time accepting responsibility.

16. Poor Self-Esteem

Poor self-esteem is lack of self-respect and self-worth. It leads to abuse of one's self and others. Ego takes the driver's seat. Decisions are taken more to satisfy the ego than to accomplish anything worthwhile. People with low self-esteem are constantly looking for identity. They are trying to find themselves. One's self is not to be found, but to be created.

Idleness and laziness are consequences of poor self-esteem and so is making excuses. Idleness is like rust that eats into the most brilliant metal.

17. Lack of Knowledge

Sixty years ago I knew everything; now I know nothing; education is a progressive discovery of our own ignorance.

— Will Durant

The first step towards knowledge is awareness of areas of ignorance. The more knowledge a person gets, the more he realizes what areas he is ignorant in. A person who thinks he knows everything has the most to learn.

Ignorant people don't know they are ignorant. They don't know that 'they don't know'. In fact, more than ignorance, the bigger problem is the illusion of knowledge, because when you think you know something—but don't—your decision-making will be flawed.

18. Fatalistic Attitude

A fatalistic attitude prevents people from accepting responsibility for their circumstances. People with fatalistic attitudes attribute success and failure to luck. They resign themselves to their fate. They accept the predestined future written in their horoscope or stars. They believe that regardless of their effort, whatever has to happen will happen. Hence they never put in any effort and complacency becomes a way of life. They wait for things to happen rather than making them happen. Success is a matter of luck, ask any failure.

Weak-minded people fall easy prey to fortune-tellers, horoscopes and self-proclaimed Godmen who are sometimes conmen. They become superstitious and ritualistic. (Some people consider a rabbit's foot lucky; but it wasn't lucky for the rabbit, was it?)

If you want to fail, believe in luck. If you want to succeed, believe in the principle of cause and effect, and you will create your own "luck". As Samuel Goldwyn said, "The harder I work, the luckier I get."

Some People Think They are Just Unlucky

This breeds a fatalistic attitude. People who get involved half-heartedly say things like:

- I will give it a try
- I will see if it works
- I will give it a shot
- I have nothing to lose
- I haven't put much into it anyway

If you think like this, you'll be sure to fail because you'll have no dedication or determination. These thinking patterns show a lack of courage, commitment and confidence. **Attempting half-heartedly is like expecting failure and achieving it.**

Effort Does It

A man bought a racehorse and put him in a barn with a big sign, "The fastest horse in the world." The owner didn't exercise the horse nor train it to keep it in good shape. He entered the horse in a race and it came last. The owner quickly changed the sign to "The fastest world for the horse." By inaction or not doing what should be done, people fail and they blame luck.

Life without vision, courage and depth is simply a blind experience. Small, lazy and weak minds always take the easiest way, the path of least resistance.

Athletes train 15 years for 15 seconds of performance. Ask them if they got lucky. Ask an athlete how he feels after a good workout. He will tell you that he feels spent. If he doesn't feel that way, it means he hasn't worked out to his maximum ability.

Losers think life is unfair. They think only of their bad breaks. They don't consider that the person who is prepared and playing well still got the same bad breaks but overcame them. That is the difference. *The winner's threshold for tolerating pain becomes higher because in the end he is not training just for the game as for his character.*

Luck Favors Those Who Help Themselves

A flood was threatening a small town and everyone was leaving for safe ground except for one man who said, "God will save me. I have faith." As the water level rose a jeep came to rescue him, the man refused, saying "God will save me. I have faith." As the water level rose further, he went up to the second story of his house, and a boat came to help him. Again he refused to go, saying, "God will save me. I have faith." The water kept rising and the man climbed on to the roof. A helicopter came to rescue him, but he said, "God will save me. I have faith." Well, finally he drowned. When he reached his Maker he angrily questioned, "I had complete faith in you. Why did you ignore my prayers and let me drown?" The Lord replied, "Who do you think sent you the jeep, the boat and the helicopter?"

The only way to overcome a fatalistic attitude is to accept responsibility and believe in the law of cause and effect rather than luck. It takes action, preparation and planning rather than waiting, wondering and wishing, to accomplish any goal in life.

Luck Shines on the Deserving

Alexander Graham Bell was desperately trying to invent a hearing aid for his partially deaf wife. He failed at inventing a hearing aid but in the process discovered the principles of the telephone. You wouldn't call someone like that lucky, would you?

Good luck is when preparation meets opportunity. Without effort and preparations, lucky coincidences don't happen.

LUCK

He worked by day
And toiled by night.
He gave up play
And some delight.
Dry books he read,
New things to learn.
And forged ahead,
Success to earn.
He plodded on with
Faith and pluck;
And when he won,
Men called it luck.

— Anonymous

19. Lack of Purpose

Great minds have purposes, others have wishes.

— Washington Irving

If we read stories of people who have overcome serious disabilities, it is evident that their burning desire to succeed was their driving force. They had a purpose in life. They wanted to prove to themselves that they could succeed in spite of all odds—and they did.

Desire is what made a paralytic Wilma Rudolph the fastest woman on the track at the 1960 Olympics, winning three gold medals.

According to Glen Cunningham, "Desire is what made a boy with burnt legs set the world record in the one-mile run."

At the age of five, a polio victim started swimming to regain strength. Because of her desire to succeed, she went on to become a world record holder at three events and won the gold at the 1956 Olympics at Melbourne. Her name is Shelley Mann.

When people lack purpose and direction, they see no opportunity. If a person has the desire to accomplish something, knows the direction to move to achieve his objective, has the dedication to stay focused, and has the discipline required to put in the hard work, then success follows. But if you don't have purpose and direction, it doesn't matter what else you have, you won't succeed.

Character is the foundation upon which all else is built. It endures.

20. Lack of Courage

Successful people do not look for miracles or easy tasks. They seek courage and strength to overcome obstacles. They look at what is left rather than what is lost. Wishes don't come true; beliefs and expectations supported by conviction do. Prayers are only answered when they are supported with courageous action. Courage and character are the critical combination for success. This is the difference between the ordinary and the extraordinary.

When our minds are filled with courage we forget our fears and overcome obstacles. Courage is not absence of fear but the overcoming of fear. Character (justice and integrity) without courage is ineffective, whereas courage without character is oppression.

A RECIPE FOR SUCCESS

Success is like baking a cake. Unless you have just the right recipe, it is not going to work. The ingredients must be of the finest quality and in the right proportions. You can't over bake it or undercook it. Once you have the correct recipe, with practice and learning from the occasional mishap, it becomes a lot easier.

You have the recipe: Whether or not to use it is your choice.

A CRASH COURSE FOR SUCCESS

- Play to win and not to lose.
- Learn from other people's mistakes.
- Associate with people of high moral character.
- Give more than you get.
- Don't look for something for nothing.
- Always think long term.
- Evaluate your strengths and build on them.
- Always keep the larger picture in mind when making a decision.
- Never compromise your integrity.

ACTION PLAN

1. Come up with three suggestions for how you can do your job better, faster, and more effectively:

   (a) _____

   _____

   _____

   (b) _____

   _____

   _____

   (c) _____

   _____

   _____

2. Write down three ways you can use the success principles in each area of your life:

    (a) Work _____

    _____

    (b) Home _____

    _____

    (c) Socially _____

    _____

3. List the areas in your life where lack of discipline is hurting you. Estimate its cost to you.

4. The next time you meet with adversity, stop and ask yourself these two questions: What can I learn from this challenge? How can I turn this lesson in life to my advantage?

5

MOTIVATION

*Motivating yourself
and others everyday*

"Good things come to those who wait, but only those things left by those who hustle."

—Abraham Lincoln

I believe in two premises: (a) most people are good people, but they can do better; and (b) most people already know what to do to improve their lives. But the question is why aren't they doing it?

What is missing is the spark—motivation. Some self-help books adopt the approach of teaching what to do; I take a different approach. I ask, "Why don't you do it?" If you ask people on the street what should be done, they will give you all the correct answers. But ask them whether they are doing it and the answer will be no. What is lacking is motivation.

The most powerful motivation comes from within our belief system. To move into action, we need to believe in what we do and accept responsibility for our life. When we accept responsibility for our behavior and actions, our attitudes toward life becomes positive. We become more productive, both personally and professionally. Our relationships improve both at home and at work. Life becomes more meaningful and fulfilling.

After a person's basic physical needs are met, emotional needs become a bigger motivator. Every behavior comes out of the "pain or gain" principle. If the pain is greater than the gain, that is a deterrent to action. If the gain is greater than the pain, that is a motivator. Gains can be tangible, such as monetary rewards, vacations and gifts. They can also be intangible, such as recognition, appreciation, sense of achievement, growth, responsibility, sense of fulfilment, self-worth, accomplishment, and belief.

LET'S DEFINE MOTIVATION

The next logical question is: what is motivation? Motivation is a drive that encourages action or feeling. To motivate means to encourage and inspire. Motivation can also mean igniting the spark for action.

Motivation is powerful. It can persuade, convince and propel you into action. In other words, motivation can be defined as motive for action. It is a force that can literally change your life.

Why do we need to get motivated?

Motivation is the driving force in our lives. It comes from a desire to succeed. Without success there is little pride in life; no enjoyment or excitement at work and at home. Life becomes like a lopsided wheel giving a bumpy ride.

The greatest enemy of motivation is complacency. Complacency leads to lack of effort, and when people are complacent they don't grow because they cannot identify what is needed in their lives.

MOTIVATION—HOW DOES IT WORK?

Once you understand what causes motivation, you can motivate yourself and achieve your goals—and you can motivate others too.

Your internal motivation is your drive and attitude. It is contagious. Your attitudes are the key to getting the response you want from others.

How does a person stay motivated and focused? One important tool that has been used by athletes for a long time is auto-suggestion. Auto-suggestions are positive statements made in the present tense and repeated regularly. In other words, it is positive self-talk. For example, let's say you're just starting a new job.

Several times each day you might say to yourself, "I feel more and more confident every day." Or let's say your teenaged son is going through a stage where everything he says seems to irritate you. You might repeat to yourself, "I will be calm and patient when I talk to John."

WHAT IS THE DIFFERENCE BETWEEN INSPIRATION AND MOTIVATION?

I conduct seminars internationally and people often ask me if I can motivate others. The answer is no, I cannot. People motivate themselves. What I can do, however, is inspire them to motivate themselves. People can create an environment that is motivating.

Inspiration is thought; motivation is action. When thinking changes it reflects in behavior. In order to inspire people to motivate themselves we need to understand their needs and wants.

What is the greatest motivator? Is it money? Recognition? Improvement in our quality of life? Acceptance by those we love? All of these can be motivating forces.

People will do a lot for money, more for a good leader, but do the most for a belief. People die for their beliefs. This happens every day, all over the world. When we believe that we are responsible for our lives and our behaviors, our outlook towards life changes for the better.

Motivation is like fire—unless you keep adding fuel to it, it dies. Your fuel is your belief in your inner values.

When this belief in inner values feeds your motivation, your motivation becomes long lasting.

INTERNAL AND EXTERNAL MOTIVATION

Motivation is classified into two types: external and internal.

External Motivation

External motivation comes from outside. Examples of external motivators are money, societal approval, fame or fear. (For example, fear of getting spanked by parents or fear of getting fired at work).

Fear Motivation

 A company wanted to set up a pension plan. In order for the plan to be implemented, it needed 100% participation. Everyone signed up except John. The plan made sense and was in the best interest of everyone. John's refusal to sign was the only obstacle. John's supervisor and other co-workers had tried, without success, to persuade him to sign.

The owner of the company called John into his office and said, "John, here is a pen and these are the papers for you to sign to enroll into the pension plan. If you don't enroll, you are fired this minute." John signed. The owner asked John why he hadn't signed earlier. John replied, "No one explained the plan quite as clearly as you did."

It is not uncommon to see the prey outsmarting the predator, because one is running for its food and the other for its life. The advantages of fear motivation are:

- It gets the job done quickly.

- It prevents losses by meeting deadlines.
- In the short run, the person's performance may improve.

We learn from history that the pyramids were built by slaves. They had to be constantly watched and reprimanded for nonperformance. The disadvantages of fear motivation are:

- It is external, which means the motivation is there while the motivator is there. When the motivator goes, the motivation also goes.
- It causes stress.
- Performance is limited to compliance.
- In the long run, performance goes down.
- It destroys creativity.
- People get used to "the stick" and then a bigger stick is needed.

People who do just enough to get by so they don't get fired will never be valuable to any organization.

A customer asked an employee, "When did you start working here?" He replied, "Ever since they threatened to fire me."

Incentive Motivation

External motivation can also take the form of incentives, bonuses, commission, recognition and so forth.

The major advantage of incentive motivation is that it works very well as long as the incentive is strong enough. Think of a donkey with a carrot dangling in front and pulling a cart behind. Incentive motivation will work if the donkey is hungry enough, the carrot is sweet enough, and the load light enough.

From time to time, you have to let the donkey take a

bite of the carrot; otherwise it is going to get discouraged. After the donkey takes a bite, its stomach is full, and you need to wait for the donkey to get hungry again before it will pull the cart. This same cycle is typically seen in our business environment. The moment sales people meet their quotas, they stop working. This is because their motivation is limited to meeting their quotas. That is external motivation, not internal.

Internal Motivation

There was a young boy who came regularly to soccer practice but never made it to the starting team. While he was practicing, his father would sit at the far end of the field, waiting for him. The matches began and for four days, the boy didn't show up for practice or the quarter- or semi-finals. He appeared for the final game, went to the coach and said, "Coach, you have always kept me in the reserves and never let me play in the games. But today, please let me play." The coach said "Son, I'm sorry, I can't let you. There are better players than you and besides, it is the finals; the reputation of the school is at stake and I cannot take a chance on you." The boy pleaded, "Coach, I promise I will not let you down. I beg of you, please let me play." The coach had never seen the boy plead like this before. He said, "Okay son, go play. But remember, I am going against my better judgment and the reputation of the school is at stake. Don't let me down."

The game started and the boy played like a house on fire. Every time he got the ball, he shot a goal. Needless to say, he was the star of the game. His team had a spectacular win.

When the game finished, the coach went up to him and

said, "Son, how could I have been so wrong? I have never seen you play like this before. What happened? How did you play so well? The boy replied, "Coach, my father is watching me today." The coach turned around and looked at the place where the boy's father used to sit. There was no one there. He said, "Son, your father used to sit there when you came for practice, but I don't see anyone there today." The boy replied, "Coach, there is something I never told you. My father was blind. Just four days ago, he died. Today is the first day he is watching me from above."

Internal motivation comes from within, such as pride, a sense of achievement, responsibility and belief.

Internal motivation is the inner gratification, not for success or winning, but for the fulfillment that comes from having done it. It is a feeling of accomplishment, rather than just achieving a goal. Reaching an unworthy goal does not produce the gratifying feeling. Internal motivation is lasting, because it comes from within and translates into self-motivation.

Motivation needs to be identified and constantly strengthened to succeed. Write down your goals. Keep them in front of you and read them morning and evening.

The two most important internal motivators are recognition and responsibility.

Recognition means being appreciated; being treated with respect and dignity; and feeling a sense of belonging.

Responsibility gives a person a feeling of belonging and ownership. He then becomes part of the bigger picture. Lack of responsibility is demotivating.

Recognition is external because it originates from

outside, through its manifestations (feelings) are internal.

Responsibility is internal as it originates from within.

Take the case of Jill, a customer service representative who had been on the job for six years, a relatively long time in a job that had a high turnover rate. Jill liked her job—she liked talking with customers and being a problem solver. What she didn't like was the fact that most of the other customer service reps, who had been there less than two years, were on equal footing with her. Jill was frustrated and discouraged that many of the other reps were not willing to listen to her suggestions. When they did have a problem, they'd go to the manager for help even though the manager didn't have the front-line experience that Jill did.

The manager began to notice that while Jill's performance wasn't bad, it wasn't as good as it had been, and Jill no longer seemed to be happy with her job. Not wanting to lose such a valuable employee, the manager gave Jill a raise. But Jill's attitude about the job did not change. While more money is always nice, what Jill was looking for was respect. When the manager finally spent some time talking with Jill and discovered the source of her dissatisfaction, the manager gave Jill the title of supervisor and told the other reps that all problems were to go through Jill. Jill's increased responsibility fueled her need for respect and her performance immediately improved.

Monetary rewards are temporary and short-lived; they are not gratifying in the long run. In contrast, seeing an idea being implemented can be emotionally grati-fying by itself. People feel that they are not being treated like objects. They feel part of a worthwhile team. The reward of doing the right thing by itself is motivating.

WE ARE ALL MOTIVATED—EITHER POSITIVELY OR NEGATIVELY

When I was in Toronto, I heard a story of two brothers. One was a drug addict and a drunk who frequently beat up his family. The other was a very successful businessman who was respected in society and had a wonderful family. How could two brothers raised by the same parents, brought up in the same environment, be so different?

The first brother was asked, "What makes you do what you do? You are a drug addict, a drunk, and you beat your family. What motivates you?" He answered, "My father. My father was a drug addict, a drunk and he beat his family. What do you expect me to be? That is what I am."

The second brother was asked, "How come you are doing everything right? What is your source of motivation?" And guess what he said? "My father. When I was a little boy, I used to see my dad drunk and doing all the wrong things. I made up my mind that that is not what I wanted to be."

Both brothers derived their motivation from the same source, but one was using it positively and the other negatively. Negative motivation brings the desire to take the easier way which ends up being the tougher way.

ON THE JOB: THE FOUR STAGES FROM MOTIVATION TO DEMOTIVATION

When people start a job, they often move through stages of motivation and competence.

1. Motivated Ineffective

When is an employee most motivated in the cycle of employment? When he joins an organization. Why?

Because he wants to prove that by hiring him, the employer made the right decision. He is motivated but because he is new to the environment. But he does not know what to do, so he is ineffective.

This is the stage when the employee is most open-minded, receptive and easy to mold to the culture of the organization. Training and orientation become imperative.

Unprofessional organizations have no, or very poor, orientation programs. The first day at the job, the supervisor shows the new employee his place of work and tells him what to do and leaves. He teaches all the bad alongwith the good that he is doing. The new employee quickly learns all the mistakes the supervisor is making because that is what he has been taught. The organization loses the opportunity to mold the individual to its culture.

Professional organizations on the other hand, take special care to induct people into their organizations. They explain to them, among other things, the following:

- The hierarchy
- Expectations of each other
- Do's and don'ts
- Parameters and guidelines
- What is acceptable and what is not
- The resources

How can one expect performance unless expectations are made clear up front? If induction and orientation are done well, many potential problems would not surface at all.

2. Motivated Effective

This is the stage when the employee has learned what to do and does it with drive and energy. He has learned the trade and it reflects in his performance. Then he moves on to the next stage.

3. Demotivated Effective

After some time the motivation level goes down and the employee starts learning the tricks of the trade. This is the stage when the employee is not motivated. He continues doing just enough so that the employer has no reason to fire him but he is really not motivated.

This stage is detrimental to growth—most people in organizations fall into this third stage. A motivated professional learns the trade and leaves the tricks to cheats and crooks, but a demotivated employee starts sabotaging the company. His performance is marginal. He makes fun of the good performers. He rejects new ideas and spreads the negativity all around.

Our objective is to bring them back to the second stage of motivated effective through training. An employee ought not to stay in the third stage too long; because from here either they move back to the second stage, which is being motivated and effective, or they move into the fourth stage.

4. Demotivated Ineffective

At this stage, the employer does not have much choice but to fire the employee, which may be the most appropriate thing to do anyway at this point.

Remember employers want the same thing as employees do. They want to succeed and improve business, and if employees help in this objective, then they make themselves valuable and achieve their own success.

DEMOTIVATING FACTORS

Why do people move from initially motivated stage to demotivated? Some of the demotivating factors are:

- Unfair criticism
- Negative criticism
- Public humiliation
- Rewarding the non-performers (which can be demotivating for the performers)
- Failure or fear of failure
- Success (which leads to complacence)
- Lack of direction
- Lack of measurable objectives
- Low self-esteem
- Lack of priorities
- Negative self-talk
- Office politics
- Unfair treatment
- Hypocrisy
- Poor standards
- Frequent change
- Responsibility without authority

A satisfied person is not necessarily a motivated person. Some people are satisfied with very little. In this case, satisfaction may lead to complacence. Motivation comes from excitement and excitement does not come unless there is full commitment.

New methods of motivation will not work till the demotivating factors are removed. Many times, just removing the demotivating factors can spark motivation.

Motivators

What we really want to accomplish is self-motivation,

when people do things for their own reasons and not yours. That is lasting motivation.

Remember the greatest motivator is belief. We have to inculcate in ourselves the belief that we are responsible for our actions and behavior. When people accept responsibility, everything improves: quality, productivity, relationships and teamwork.

A few steps to motivate others:

- Give recognition
- Give respect
- Make work interesting
- Be a good listener
- Encourage goal setting
- Provide opportunities for growth
- Provide training
- Throw a challenge
- Help, but don't do for others what they should do for themselves

Conclusion

People do things for their own reasons, not yours. This is illustrated by a story about Ralph Waldo Emerson. He and his son once were struggling to get a calf into the barn. Both father and son were exhausted, pulling and pushing. A little girl was passing by. She put her little finger into the calf's mouth, allowing it to suck, and the calf lovingly followed her to the barn.

ACTION PLAN

Everyone who's ever taken a shower has an idea. It's the person who gets out, dries off, and does something about it who makes a difference.

— Nolan Bushnell

1. Develop a sense of pride through training.
2. Reward performance.
3. Set well-defined, clear goals.
4. Set high expectations.
5. Set clear, measurable benchmarks.
6. Evaluate the needs of others.
7. Make others part of your big picture.
8 Set a good example by being a positive role model.
9. Build the self-esteem of others.

6

SELF-ESTEEM

Building a positive attitude

What a man thinks of himself: that is what determines, or rather indicates, his fate.

— Henry David Thoreau

 A beggar was sitting at a train station with a bowl full of pencils. A young executive passed by and dropped a dollar into the bowl, but didn't take any pencils. He then boarded the train. Just before the doors were to close, the executive suddenly exited the train and went back to the beggar. He grabbed a bunch of pencils, and said, "I will take some pencils. They are priced right. After all, you are a business person and so am I," and he dashed back on to the train.

Six months later, the executive attended a party. The beggar was also there, dressed in a suit and tie. The beggar recognized the executive, went up to him, and said, "You probably don't recognize me, but I remember you." He then narrated the incident that had happened six months before. The executive said, "Now that you remind me, I do recall that you were begging. What are you doing here in a suit and tie?" The beggar replied, "You probably don't know what you did for me that day. Instead of giving me charity, you treated me with dignity. You grabbed the bunch of pencils and said, 'They are priced right. After all, you are a business person and so am I.' After you left, I thought to myself—what am I doing here? Why am I begging? I decided to do something constructive with my life. I packed my bag, started working and here I am. I just want to thank you for giving me back my dignity. That incident changed my life."

WHAT changed in the beggar's life? What changed was that his self-esteem went up and so did his performance. This is the magic of self-esteem in our lives.

Simply, self-esteem is how we feel about ourselves.

Our opinion of ourselves critically influences everything, from our performance at work, our relationships and our role as parents, to our accomplishments in life. Self-esteem is a major component in determining success or failure. High self-esteem leads to a happy, gratifying and purposeful life. Unless you perceive yourself as worthwhile, you cannot have high self-esteem. Self-esteem gives you internal drive. All great world leaders and teachers throughout history have concluded that one must be internally driven in order to be a success.

We transfer our unconscious self-appraisal to others and they respond to us accordingly. People with high self-esteem grow in conviction, competence and willingness to accept responsibility. They face life with optimism, have better relationships and more fulfilling lives. They are motivated and ambitious. They are more sensitive. Their performance and risk-taking ability go up. They are open to new opportunities and challenges. They can give and receive criticism and compliments, tactfully and with ease.

Self-esteem is a feeling that comes from the awareness of what is good and having done it.

Self-Esteem is Our Self-Concept

There is a story about a farmer who planted pumpkins on his land. For no reason, he put a small pumpkin, hanging by the vine, into a glass jar.

At harvest time, he saw that the pumpkin had grown, equivalent only to the shape and size of the jar. Just as the pumpkin could not grow beyond the boundaries restricting it, you cannot perform beyond the boundaries of your self-concept, whatever those boundaries may be.

SOME ADVANTAGES OF HIGH SELF-ESTEEM

There is a direct relationship between people's feelings and their productivity. High self-esteem is evident in respect for one's self, others, property, law, parents and one's country. The reverse is also true.

High Self-Esteem:

- Builds strong conviction.
- Creates willingness to accept responsibility.
- Builds optimistic attitudes.
- Leads to better relationships and fulfilling lives.
- Develops a caring attitude and makes a person more sensitive to others' needs.
- Makes a person self-motivated and ambitious.
- Makes a person open to new opportunities and challenges.
- Improves performance and increases risk-taking ability.
- Helps a person give and receive both criticism and compliments tactfully and easily.
- Prefers loss of business to loss of credibility because they realize that one cannot put a price on one's credibility.

Low Self-Esteem

How do we recognize poor self-esteem? What are the behavior patterns of a person with poor self-esteem? The following is a brief list that is not all inclusive but is indicative.

- They are generally gossipmongers.
- They have a critical nature. They criticize as if there

is a contest going on to see who can criticize the most.

- They are concerned about egos—they are arrogant—and pretend they know it all. People with low self-esteem are generally difficult to work with and work for. They tear down others to get a feeling of superiority.
- They are closed minded and self-centered.
- They constantly make excuses—always justifying failures.
- They never accept responsibility—always blaming others.
- They have a fatalistic attitude—they have no initiative and always wait for things to happen.
- They are jealous by nature.
- They are unwilling to accept positive criticism. They become defensive.
- They are bored and uncomfortable when alone.
- Poor self-esteem leads to a breakdown in decency. People with low self-esteem don't know where to draw the line—where decency stops and vulgarity starts. It is not unusual for people to tell jokes at social get-togethers, but with every drink, the jokes get dirtier and dirtier.
- They don't have genuine friends because they are not genuine themselves.
- They make promises they know they are not going to keep. A person with low self-esteem would promise the moon to make a sale. Promises not kept lead to loss of credibility.
- Their behavior is senseless and erratic. They swing from one end of the pendulum to another. They may be all sugar and honey today but the same

people may be out to cut your throat tomorrow. They lack balance.

- They alienate people and tend to be lonely.
- They are touchy by nature—this is called the fragile ego. Anytime something is said, a person with a fragile ego takes it personally and gets hurt. It leads to dejection.

What is the difference between being touchy and being sensitive? Touchiness is the cactus approach: Touch me and I will hurt you. Being sensitive is the positive approach, the caring approach. Many times the two are used interchangeably. People say be careful when talking to so and so, he or she is very sensitive. What they are really saying is that the person is touchy, so be careful.

- They have negative expectations of themselves and others and are seldom disappointed in those expectations.
- They lack confidence.
    1. They constantly seek approval and validation from others. Seeking approval is different from seeking a second opinion, which really means consultation.
    2. They brag about themselves—a sign of lack of confidence.
    3. They exhibit submissive or timid behavior. These are the people who constantly apologize for their existence. They are always putting themselves down, which is different from being humble. Humility comes from confidence whereas putting yourself down comes from lack of it. A person who lacks confidence cannot be an effective

leader. Others sense this lack of confidence, which results in a lack of respect.

4. They lack assertiveness. People with low self-esteem are not willing to stand up for their beliefs. On the other hand, being unduly aggressive is also a sign of poor self-esteem. Being aggressive in situations that require compassion does not amount to assertiveness.

5. Their lack of confidence results in conformist behavior. The thinking is, if everybody is doing it, then I should too. Every day we see people giving in to peer pressure, knowing full well what they are doing could be detrimental to themselves or others, yet they do it to be accepted. People with low self-esteem go along to get along. They are looking for outside validation because they lack confidence in themselves.

6. They try to "keep up with the Joneses". When people buy houses, cars and other possessions, and participate in activities to impress others, they often spend money they haven't earned and buy things they don't need or like. All of this is an attempt to impress others – others whom they don't necessarily like or admire.

7. They exhibit Nonconformist or attention-seeking behavior. In order to gain attention, people with poor self-esteem might do senseless things just to stand out and be noticed. They get a "kick" and a sense of importance from perversion. Some people choose to do wrong and be wrong just to be different and gain attention. Examples are people who brag excessively, the classroom

clown, people who dress flamboyantly, and so forth.

- They are indecisive and do not accept responsibility. Lack of courage and fear of criticism lead to indecisive behavior.
- They rebel against authority. I make a distinction between rebelling out of the courage of one's convictions and rebelling because of poor self-esteem. All the great world leaders, such as Mahatma Gandhi, Martin Luther King and Abraham Lincoln were rebels. They rebelled against authority out of the courage of their convictions; a person with low self-esteem rebels against authority just because it is authority, even when the authority is right.
- They are anti-social and may be withdrawn.
- They lack a sense of direction and have an "I don't care" attitude that is reflected in their behavior.
- They have a hard time giving or receiving compliments. In giving they feel they might be misconstrued and in receiving they feel they are undeserving. Feeling unworthy is not humility.
- They place too much emphasis on material things. People with poor self-esteem judge your worth by your possessions, not by who you are. They look at what kind of car you drive, what kind of home you live in, and what kind of clothes and jewelry you wear. They forget that people make things and not vice versa. People with poor self-esteem place more emphasis on net worth than self-worth. Their lives revolve around ads and fads. Designer labels are their

status symbols. Take away their possessions and they will die of shame. They get into a rat race. As Lily Tomlin said, "The problem with the rat race is that even if you win, you are still a rat."

- They show a lack of pride in themselves—they are uncouth.
- They are takers, not givers.

Low self-esteem could lead to extremes of behavior. A person with high self-esteem could choose identical behavior for different reasons. He may be alone because he prefers solitude, whereas a person with low self-esteem prefers to be alone because he is uncomfortable in groups.

Here are some comparison characteristics of people with high and low self-esteem:

High Self-Esteem	*Low Self-Esteem*
Talk about ideas	Talk about people
Caring attitude	Critical attitude
Humility	Arrogance
Respects authority	Rebels against authority
Courage of conviction	Goes along to get along
Confidence	Confusion
Concerned about character	Concerned about reputation
Assertive	Aggressive
Accepts responsibility	Blames the whole world
Self-interest	Selfish
Optimistic	Fatalistic
Understanding	Greedy
Willing to learn	Know it all
Sensitive	Touchy
Solitude	Lonely
Discuss	Argue

Believes in self-worth	Believes in net worth only
Guided	Misguided
Discipline	Distorted sense of freedom
Internally driven	Externally driven
Respects others	Looks down on others
Enjoys decency	Enjoys vulgarity
Knows limit	Everything goes
Giver	Taker

The objective of this list is to provide a basis for self-evaluation, not to produce guilt. It is not necessary to have all the high self-esteem traits. Some characteristics may be present to a greater or lesser degree. So long as we are able to recognize our goals, we can make an effort to improve ourselves.

WHY PUT ON A MASK?

A young executive with poor self-esteem was promoted but he couldn't reconcile himself to his new office and position. There was a knock at his door. To show how important and busy he was, he picked up the phone and then asked the visitor to come in. As the man waited for the executive, the executive kept talking on the phone, nodding and saying, "No problem, I can handle that." After a few minutes he hung up and asked the visitor what he could do for him. The man replied, "Sir, I'm here to connect your phone."

What is the Message?

Why pretend? What are we trying to prove? What do we want to accomplish? Why do we need to lie? Why look for feelings of false importance? All of these types of behavior comes from insecurity and poor self-esteem.

Why Pretend?

Our character can be judged by everything we do or don't do, like or don't like. Our character is revealed by:

- The kind of company we keep or avoid.
- How we treat others. Especially our subordinates, the elderly and the disabled.
- Our choice of books, music and movies.
- The kind of jokes we tell or laugh at.

Every action of ours gives us away anyway, so why pretend? I believe that if a person lives with conviction, sensitivity and cooperation, he can move others with his effort. That person becomes worthy of self-respect.

Positive Self-Esteem	*Negative Self-Esteem*
1. self-respect	self-put-down
2. self-confidence	self-doubt
3. self-worth	self-abuse
4. self-acceptance	self-denial
5. self-love	self-centeredness
6. self-knowledge	self-deceit
7. self-discipline	self-indulgence

Self-esteem is the way we feel about ourselves. Self-image is the way we see ourselves. When we feel good the world looks nice, productivity goes up and relationships are a lot better. The reverse is just as true.

High self-esteem does not mean having a big ego. Unless a person is at peace with himself, he cannot be at peace with others, just as we cannot give to others what we don't have. Unless we possess the components of self-esteem, we cannot share it with others. We need to first evaluate ourselves honestly and put ourselves in order. Even in an aircraft, the safety instructions tell you to put on your oxygen mask first before helping your child. This is not selfishness. You need to be strong physically to help others physically and you need to be strong emotionally before you can give to others emotionally.

CAUSES OF LOW SELF-ESTEEM

We start forming our self-esteem, positive or negative, from the day we are born. We develop feelings about ourselves that are reinforced by others.

Negative Self-Talk or Negative Auto-suggestions

Negative self-talk is when we say to ourselves, consciously or unconsciously, statements such as:

- I have a poor memory.
- I'm not good at math.
- I'm not an athlete.
- I'm tired.

Such statements only reinforce the negative and put us down. Very soon our minds start believing these statements and our behavior changes accordingly. They become self-fulfilling prophecies.

Environment

Home

The greatest gift a parent can give his children are roots. The best part of a family tree is the roots. Noticing a little girl's courteous and polite behavior, the teacher asked, "Who taught you to be so courteous and polite?" The girl replied, "No one. It just runs in our family."

Upbringing

"Fellow citizens, why do you turn and scrape every stone to gather wealth and take so little care of your children to whom one day, you must relinquish it all?"

— Socrates

In order for our children to turn out well, we need to spend twice the time and half the money. It is less painful to learn in youth than be ignorant as adults?

Parents with high self-esteem, breed confidence and high self-esteem in their children by giving them positive concepts, beliefs and values. The reverse is also true.

It is a great heritage to have honest parents. Parents who participate in crooked business deals unfortunately set bad examples for their future generations.

A strong role model or mentor could be a parent, relative or teacher who is held in high regard. During their formative years, children look up to adults in positions of influence. Even as adults, we look to our supervisors and managers as role models.

*LITTLE EYES UPON YOU**

There are little eyes upon you
and they're watching night and day.
There are little ears that quickly
take in every word you say.
There are little hands all eager
to do anything you do;

---

*From *The Moral Compass*, edited by William J. Bennett, Simon & Schuster, New York, 1995, pp. 523-24.

And a little boy who's dreaming
of the day he'll be like you.
You're the little fellow's idol,
you're the wisest of the wise.
In his little mind about you
no suspicions ever rise.
He believes in you devoutly,
holds all that you say and do;
He will say and do, in your way,
when he's grown up like you.
There's a wide-eyed little fellow
who believes you're always right;
And his eyes are always opened,
and he watches day and night.
You are setting an example
every day in all you do,
For the little boy who's waiting
to grow up to be like you.

What Makes a Child Delinquent?

- Teach him to put a price tag on everything and he will put his integrity for sale.
- Teach him never to take a stand and then he will fall for anything.
- Make him believe that winning is not everything, that it is the only thing and he will make every effort to win by hook or by crook.
- Give a child everything he wants right from infancy and he will grow up believing that the world owes him a living and everything will be handed to him on a platter.
- When he picks up bad language, laugh at him. This will make him think he is cute.

- Don't ever give him any moral or ethical values. Wait until he is 21 and let him "determine his own."
- Give him choices without direction. Never teach him that every choice has a consequence.
- Never tell him he is wrong he might develop a complex. This will condition him to believe that society is against him when he gets arrested for doing something wrong.
- Always pick up things that he leaves lying around—books, shoes, clothes and so on. Do everything for him so that he will learn to push all responsibilities onto others.
- Let him read, watch and hear anything he wants. Be careful what he feeds his body, but let his mind feed on garbage.
- In order to be popular with his peers, he must go along to get along.
- Quarrel frequently when he is present. This way he won't be surprised when things fall apart at home.
- Give him as much money as he wants. Never teach him respect for the value of money. Make sure he does not have things as tough as you did.
- Provide instant gratification for all sensual desires such as food, drink and comfort. Deprivation can cause frustration.
- Side with him against neighbors and teachers, as they are prejudiced against him.
- When he gets into real trouble, excuse yourself by saying, "I tried my best but could never do anything with him."
- Don't put your foot down because you believe discipline takes away freedom.

- Prefer remote control to parental control in order to teach independence.

CHILDREN LEARN WHAT THEY LIVE

If a child lives with criticism, he learns to condemn.
If a child lives with praise, he learns to appreciate.
If a child lives with hostility, he learns to fight.
If a child lives with tolerance, he learns to be patient.
If a child lives with ridicule, he learns to be shy.
If a child lives with encouragement, he learns confidence.
If a child lives with shame, he learns to feel guilty.
If a child lives with approval, he learns to like himself.
If a child lives with fairness, he learns justice.
If a child lives with security, he learns to have faith.
If a child lives with acceptance and friendship,
he learns to find love in the world.

What children get, they give to society.

BUILDING SELF-CONFIDENCE

A young couple used to leave their daughter at a day-care center every day before going to work. As they parted company, the parents and child kissed each other's hands and then put the kisses in their pockets. All during the day when the little girl got lonely she would take out a kiss and put it on her cheek. This little routine made them feel together even though they were physically apart. What a wonderful thought.

Education

Being ignorant is not shameful, but being unwilling to learn is. Role models can teach through example.

Children who are taught the importance of integrity during their formative years generally don't lose it. It becomes a part of life, which is what we are looking for in any professional, whether a contractor, attorney, accountant, politician, police officer or judge. Integrity is a lot stronger than honesty. In fact it is the foundation of honesty.

Youth are impressionable. When they see their mentors—such as parents, teachers or political leaders—cheating with pride or bragging about petty dishonesty such as stealing a towel in a hotel or cutlery from the restaurants, the following happens:

- They are disappointed.
- They lose respect for their mentors.
- Constant exposure breeds acceptance in them.

POOR ROLE MODELS

A school teacher asked a little boy what his father did for a living. The boy replied, "I'm not sure, but I guess he makes pens, pencils, light bulbs, toilet paper rolls, because that is what he brings home every day in his lunch box."

Making Unfair Comparison

Fair comparisons are okay, but unfair comparisons make a person feel inferior. Comparing yourself to others basically brings out the competitive spirit to outperform the next person. People with high self-esteem don't compete with others; instead, they improve their own performance. They compete against themselves. They compare their performance against their capabilities.

Failure or Success: A Ripple Effect

There is a lot of truth in the statement, "success breeds success and failure breeds failure." In sports, we often see that whenever the champion's morale is low—and it does get low at some point—the coach will never put him up against a good fighter because if he suffers one more defeat, his self-esteem will go even lower. To bring his self-confidence back, the coach pits him against a weaker opponent and that victory raises his self-esteem. A slightly stronger opponent is next and that victory brings up the level of confidence, and on and on until the day comes when the champion is ready to face the ultimate challenge.

With every success, self-confidence goes up and it is easier to succeed the next time. For this reason, any good leader, be it a parent, teacher or supervisor, would start a child off with easy tasks. With every successful completion, the child's level of confidence and self-esteem goes up. Add to that positive strokes—encouragement, and this will start solidifying positive self-esteem. Our responsibility is to help break the chain of failure and put ourselves and our children into the chain of success.

Confusing Failing with Failure

Success is 99 percent failure

— Soichiro Honda (founder, Honda Motor Corporation)

When people fail in any particular event, most get so disheartened that they start looking at themselves as failures, not realizing that failing does not equal failure. I might have failed but I am not a failure. I may be fooled but I am not a fool. You are a failure only when you quit.

Unrealistic Expectations of Perfection by Parents, Teachers and Supervisors

Suppose a child comes home with a report card with five As and one B usually the first thing his parents will say is, "Why the B?" Should the parents congratulate the child for the B and accept a lower standard? Not at all.

What the child is really looking for is acknowledgment and encouragement for the effort in getting the five As. Parents, after acknowledging and praising the As, can make clear their expectations of seeing all six As and offer help if needed. If we lower our standards, the chances are pretty good that the performance next time would drop to those expectations.

Similarly at work, an employee can do hundred things right and one thing wrong. Guess what the boss chooses to comment on. Acknowledge the positive, but don't lower your standards.

Lack of Discipline

What is Discipline?

Does discipline mean corrective action after a problem occurs or a wrong is done? Is it imposition? Is it abuse? Does it take away freedom?

The answer is none of the above. Discipline does not mean that a person takes a belt and beats up kids. That is madness. Discipline is loving firmness. It is direction. It is prevention before a problem arises. It is harnessing and channeling energy for great performance. Discipline is not something you do to others, but something you do for those you care about.

Discipline is an act of love. Sometimes you have to be unkind to be kind: Not all medicines are sweet, nor all surgeries painless, but we have to use it. We need to learn from nature. We are all familiar with that big animal, the giraffe. A mama giraffe gives birth to a baby giraffe standing. All of a sudden, the baby falls on a hard surface from the cushion of mama's womb, and sits on the ground. The first thing mama does is to get behind the baby and give him a hard kick. The baby gets up, but his legs are weak and wobbly and the baby falls down. Mama goes behind again and gives him one more kick. The baby gets up but sits down again. Mama keeps kicking till the baby gets on its feet and starts moving. Why? Because mama knows that the only chance of survival for the baby is to get on its feet—otherwise it will be eaten by predators.

My question to you is: Is this an act of love? You bet it is.

Children brought up in a loving, disciplined environment end up respecting their parents more and become law-abiding citizens. The reverse is just as true.

If discipline were practiced in every home, juvenile delinquency would be reduced by 95%.

—J. Edgar Hoover

Good parents are not afraid to enforce discipline because of momentary dislikes by children.

Discipline Gives Freedom

Our instinct is to do whatever we want regardless of the consequences. Allowing a child to eat a box of chocolates could lead to sickness. On the other hand, the discipline of eating one or two pieces a day produces an enjoyable experience for a longer time.

Freedom is not procured by a full enjoyment of what is desired but controlling the desire.

— Epictetus

There is a misconception that freedom means doing your own thing. One cannot always have what one desires. Many times it is not easy to comprehend the benefits of good values and discipline. It may even seem more profitable, enjoyable and convenient to do otherwise. All we need to do is see countless instances where lack of discipline has prevented people from succeeding.

Rather than the restraints of discipline pulling us down, discipline is really taking us up. That is what discipline is all about.

A boy was flying a kite with his father and asked him what kept the kite up. Dad replied, "The string." The boy said, "Dad, it is the string that is holding the kite down." The father asked his son to watch as he broke the string.

Guess what happened to the kite? It came down. Isn't that true in life? Sometimes the very things that we think are holding us down are the things that are helping us fly. That is what discipline is all about.

I Want to Be Free

We hear this phrase all the time: "I want to be free."If you take the train off the track, it is free, but where does it go? If everyone could make their own traffic laws and drive on any side of the road would you call that freedom or chaos? What is missing is discipline. By observing the rules, we are actually gaining freedom.

Discipline is Loving Firmness

I have asked this question to many participants in my seminars: "If your child had a fever of 105°F and did not want to go to the doctor, what would you do?" Invariably they said they would get medical help even if the child resisted. Why? Because it is in the best interest of the child.

Parenting is Not a Popularity Contest

A judge, when sentencing a man for robbery, asked if he had anything to say. The man replied, "Yes your honor. Please sentence my parents to jail also." The judge asked, "Why?" The prisoner answered, "When I was a little boy, I stole a pencil from school. My parents knew about it but never said a word. Then I stole a pen. They knowingly ignored it. I continued to steal many other things from the school and the neighborhood till it became an obsession. They knew about it, yet they never said a word. If anyone belongs in jail with me, they do."

He is right. Although it does not absolve him of his responsibility, the question is did the parents do their job right? Obviously not.

Giving choices to children is important, but choices without direction result in disaster. Complete mental and physical preparation is the result of sacrifice and self-discipline.

Parents spend an average of 15 minutes a week in "meaningful dialog" with their children—children who are left to glean whatever values they can from peers and TV.

— Journal of the American Family Association

Ask yourself: Without discipline,

- can a captain run a ship effectively?
- can an athlete win a game?
- can a violinist play well at a concert?

The answer is, "Of course not." To each of the above questions. Why then do we question today whether discipline is necessary in matters of personal conduct or to achieve any standard? It is absolutely necessary.

Today the philosophy is: "If it feels good, do it." I have heard parents innocently saying, "I don't care what my kids do so long as it makes them happy. That is all that matters." I ask them, "Wouldn't you want to know what makes them happy?" If beating people up on the streets and taking their things away are what make them happy, there is a word in the English language for them, it is called "perversion."

How and where we derive our happiness from is just as important as the happiness itself. It is a result of our values, discipline and responsibility.

We keep hearing "do what you like." The reverse is just as true. Like what you do. Many times we need to do what ought to be done whether we like it or not.

A mother comes home after a long day's work, takes care of the household chores, looks after the baby and goes to sleep exhausted. In the middle of the night the baby cries. Does mama feel like getting up? No, but she gets up anyway. Why? For three reasons:

- Love
- Duty
- Responsibility

We cannot live our lives by emotions alone. We need to add discipline, no matter what age we are. Winning in life comes when we do not succumb to what we want to do but do what ought to be done. That requires discipline.

Labeling and Put-Downs by Parents, Teachers and Supervisors

Have you heard some parents playfully or affectionately calling their kids "dummy" and "stupid"? Labels stick for life. When the kids grow up they will be sure to prove the parents right. Labels do not only stick for life but for generations. The caste system in India is a prime example of how labeling can hurt. Upper caste or lower caste, "If it is not a label, what is it?"

Common put-downs parents say to their kids are:

- You are dumb.
- You never do anything right.
- You will never amount to anything.

Teaching the Right Values

Many times, inadvertently and innocently, we end up teaching wrong values within our families and organizations. For example, we tell our children or staff to lie for us.

- Tell them I am not here.
- The check is in the mail.

We all look to our parents, teachers and supervisors to teach us integrity. And many times we are disappointed. Practicing these petty lies turns a person into a professional liar. When we teach others to lie for us, a day will come when they will lie to us too. For example, a secretary calls in sick when she really wants to go shopping. Maybe the boss gave her enough practice lying for him that she has become an expert in lying to him.

STEPS TO BUILDING A POSITIVE SELF-ESTEEM

Turn Scars into Stars

Read the life histories of people who have turned a negative into a positive, adversity into advantage, stumbling blocks into stepping stones. They refuse to let disappointment and failures pull them down.

Some of the best music was composed by Beethoven. What was his handicap? He was deaf. Some of the best poetry written on nature was written by Milton. What was his handicap? He was blind. One of the greatest world leaders was US President Franklin D. Roosevelt. What was his handicap? He served from a wheelchair.

THE WILMA RUDOLPH STORY*

Wilma Rudolph was born into a poor home in Tennessee. At age four, she had double pneumonia with scarlet fever, a deadly combination which left her paralyzed with polio. She had to wear a brace and the doctor said she would never put her foot on the earth. But her mother encouraged her; she told Wilma that with God-given ability, persistence and faith she could do anything she wanted. Wilma said, "I want to be the fastest woman on the track on this earth." At the age of nine, against the advice of the doctors, she removed the brace and took the first step the doctors had said she never would. At the age of 13, she entered her first race and

---

*Adapted from *Star Ledger*, November 13, 1994.

came way, way last. And then she entered her second, and third and fourth and came way, way last until a day came when she came in first.

At the age of 15 she went to Tennessee State University where she met a coach by the name of Ed Temple. She told him, "I want to be the fastest woman on the track on this earth." Temple said, "With your spirit nobody can stop you and besides, I will help you."

The day came when she was at the Olympics and at the Olympics you are matched with the best of the best. Wilma was matched against a woman named Jutta Heine who had never been beaten. The first event was the 100-meter race. Wilma beat Jutta Heine and won her first gold medal. The second event was the 200-meter race and Wilma beat Jutta a second time and won her second gold medal. The third event was the 400-meter relay and she was racing against Jutta one more time. In the relay, the fastest person always runs the last lap and they both anchored their teams. The first three people ran and changed the baton easily. When it came to Wilma's turn, she dropped the baton. But Wilma saw Jutta shoot up at the other end; she picked the baton, ran like a machine, beat Jutta a third time and won her third gold medal. It became history: That a paralytic woman became the fastest woman on this earth at the 1960 Olympics.

What a lesson to be learnt from Wilma. It teaches us that successful people do it in spite of, not in absence of, problems.

When we hear or read stories of people who have turned adversity into opportunity, doesn't it motivate us? If we regularly read biographies and autobiographies of such people, won't we stay motivated?

Learn Intelligent Ignorance

Education teaches us what we can do and also teaches us what we cannot do.

I'm looking for a lot of men with an infinite capacity for not knowing what cannot be done.

— Henry Ford

Henry Ford gave this world the V8 engine. He did not have much formal education. In fact, he did not go to school beyond the age of 14. He was intelligent enough to know that a V8 engine would be of great value to his company but he didn't know how to build it. So he asked all his highly educated or qualified people to build one. According to them, a V8 was impossible to build. But Henry Ford insisted on having his V8. A few months later he asked his people if they had the V8 and they replied, "We know what can be done and we also know what cannot be done. The V8 is an impossibility." This went on for many months and still Henry Ford said, "I want my V8." And shortly thereafter the same people who said it was impossible produced his V8 engine.

Why? They let their imagination run beyond academic limitation. Education teaches us what can be done and sometimes also teaches us false limitations.

THE BUMBLEBEE

We need to learn from nature. According to scientists, the bumblebee's body is too heavy and its wingspan too small for it to be able to fly. But the bumblebee doesn't know that and it keeps flying.

When you don't know your limitations, you go out and surprise yourself. In hindsight, you wonder if you had any limitations to begin with. The only limitations a person has are those that are self-imposed. Don't let education put limitations on you.

Do Something for Others Who Cannot Repay You in Cash or Kind

Dr. Karl Menninger, a world-renowned psychiatrist, was once asked, "What would you advise someone if you knew that person was going to have a nervous breakdown?" The audience expected Dr. Menninger to advise consulting a professional. But he didn't. He said, "I would advise that person to go to the other side of town, find someone in need, and help that person. By doing that, we get out of our own way." A lot of times we get in our own way, don't we?

Be a volunteer. It builds self-worth. Helping others as you would expect others to help you gives a feeling of gratification. The process of giving without having expectations or getting anything in return raises one's self-esteem.

A healthy personality has the need not only to get but also to give.

Learn to Give and Receive Compliments

Don't miss out on any opportunity to give sincere compliments. Remember, the key word is sincerity. When others give you a compliment, accept it graciously and gracefully with two words, "Thank you." That is a sign of humility.

Accept Responsibility

We need to accept responsibility for our behavior and our actions and insulate ourselves from excuses. Don't be like the student who failed just because he didn't like the teacher or the subject. Who is he hurting the most? We have to accept responsibility and stop blaming others. Then, and only then, will productivity and quality of life improve.

> *Our privileges can be no greater than our obligations. The protection of our rights can endure no longer than the performance of our responsibilities.*
>
> — John F. Kennedy

Excuses make the problem worse than the problem itself.

We owe responsibility

- to self
- to family
- to work
- to society
- to the environment

We can add to the greenery by planting trees, stopping soil erosion and preserving natural beauty.

We cannot live as if we have another earth we can move to. On a daily basis, we need to do something that makes this world a better place to live. We are custodians for the future generations. If we do not behave responsibly, how can future generations forgive us?

If the average life expectancy of a person is 75 years and if you are 40 years old, you have 365 days x 35 years, to live. Ask yourself this question: What are you going to do with this time? When we accept or add responsibility, we make ourselves more valuable.

Practice Discipline

Self-discipline does not kill joy but builds it. You see people with talent and ability, and yet they are unsuccessful. They are frustrated and the same behavior pattern affects their business, their health, and their relationships with others. They are dissatisfied and blame it on luck without realizing that many problems are caused by lack of discipline.

Set Goals

Well-defined goals give a person a sense of direction, a feeling of accomplishment when he reaches his goals. More important than goals is a sense of purpose and vision. They give meaning and fulfillment to life.

What we get upon achieving our goals is a lot less important than what we become. It is the process of becoming that gives us a good feeling. That is what self-esteem is all about.

In goal-setting, we need to be realistic. Unrealistic goals remain unaccomplished, leading to poor self-esteem, whereas realistic goals are encouraging and build high self-esteem.

Associate with People of High Moral Character

Associate yourself with people of good quality if you esteem your reputation, for it is better to be alone than to be in bad company.

— George Washington

Test of Friendship

Negative influences come in the form of peer pressure. People say, "Aren't you my friend?" Remember, true friends never want to see their friends hurt.

If I ever saw that a friend had had one drink too many, I would put my foot down and not let him drive. I would rather lose the friendship than lose a friend.

It is common to see people doing wrong things to get

accepted, saying, "it is cool," not realizing they will be left cold.

What starts as peer pressure may be in reality a test of friendship. Where will they be when you are in trouble? How far will they go to help you? And the biggest question is: If they don't have the character today, how will they have the character tomorrow to help you? Associating with people of high moral character helps build self-esteem.

Peer Pressure

When the desire to belong to the herd becomes stronger than the desire to stand up for what is right, it is evident that what is lacking is courage and character. Going along to get along is a safer path, keeps one's peers happy, and one does not risk being laughed at. That is where people with high self-esteem draw the line. That is what separates the men from the boys.

Examples:

- School kids conform because they do not want to be laughed at.
- Students don't give the answers because others will make fun of them.
- Factory workers keep performance low to keep peers happy.

Moderation

Many people say, "Moderation is OK. I try a little and quit." The question is, "In moderation, is it really okay?"

- To cheat?
- To lie?
- To steal?

- To take drugs?
- To have illicit affairs?

Some people frequently rationalize, "I can quit whenever I want." They don't realize that negative influences are more powerful than will-power.

Become Internally Driven, Not Externally Driven

One day, if someone gets up on the right side of the bed and calls me and says, "You are the greatest person on earth. You are doing a great job and I want you to know I am honored to call you a friend," I know he is sincere. How does it make me feel? Great. But the next day, he gets up on the wrong side of the bed, picks up the phone and says, "You rascal, you cheat, you crook! You are the biggest fraud in town." How does it make me feel? Terrible.

So the first day when he says "you are the greatest guy," I feel great and the next day when he says "you rascal," I feel terrible. Who is controlling my life? Obviously, he is. Is that the way I want to go through life? Not at all. That is being externally driven.

I want to be internally driven. When he calls me and says I am the greatest guy, it is good to hear those words. But even if he doesn't say those words, in my own estimation, I am still a good human being. And the next day when he rips me apart, while his words may initially sting, he can't bring me down, because in my own estimation, I am a good human being. When a person makes statements like, "You make me angry," the focus of control is external. But if he says, "I am angry" or "I choose to be angry", the focus is internal.

No one can make you feel inferior without your permission.

— Eleanor Roosevelt

There is a story about an ancient Indian sage who was called ugly names by a passerby. The sage listened unperturbed till the man ran out of words. He asked the man, "If an offering is not accepted, who does it belong to?" The man replied, "It belongs to the person who offered it." The sage said, "I refuse to accept your offering," and walked away, leaving the man dazed. The sage was internally driven.

So long as we blame outside sources, our miseries will continue and we will feel helpless. Unless we accept responsibility for our feelings and behavior, we cannot change. The first step is to ask:

- Why did I get upset?
- Why am I angry?
- Why am I depressed?

Then we start getting the clues to overcome them. Happiness is a result of positive self-esteem. If you ask people what makes them happy, you will get all kinds of answers. Most of them would include material things but that is not really true. Happiness comes from being and not having. One can have everything in life and yet not be happy. The reverse is also true.

Happiness is internal. Happiness is like a butterfly. If you run after it, it keeps flying away. If you stand still, it comes and sits on your shoulder.

Develop a Mindset That Brings Happiness

Bitterness is a sign of emotional failure. It paralyzes our capacity to do good. Set your own standards. Be honest to yourself. Compete against yourself. Do the following:

- Look for the positive in every person and in every situation.

- Resolve to be happy.
- Set your own standards judiciously.
- Develop an immunity to negative criticism.
- Learn to find pleasure in every little thing.
- Remember all times are not the same. Ups and downs are part of life.
- Make the best of every situation.
- Keep yourself constructively occupied.
- Help others less fortunate than yourself.
- Learn to get over things. Don't brood.
- Forgive yourself and others. Don't hold guilt or bear grudges.

Give Yourself Positive Auto-suggestions

Develop the habit of giving yourself positive self-talk. Auto-suggestions alter your belief system by influencing your subconscious mind. Your behavior reflects your belief system. Hence, auto-suggestions affect your behavior by influencing your belief system. It becomes a self-fulfilling prophecy. Examples:

- I can handle it.
- I can do it.
- I am good at math.
- I have a good memory.

Our Greatest Strength Can Become
Our Greatest Weakness

Any strength overextended becomes a weakness. For example, in sales, good speaking ability is a strength. It is not uncommon to see salespeople with good speaking ability talk themselves into a sale, then talk too much and talk themselves right out of the sale. Their strength got them into it; however, overextended, it became a weakness and they lose the sale.

Listening is a strength. Overextended, however, it could mean that a person listens a lot but does not speak enough. It becomes a weakness.

Our Greatest Weakness Can Become Our Greatest Strength

Anger is a weakness. How can it be turned into a strength? One lady demonstrated by getting MADD! MADD stands for Mothers Against Drunk Driving. This woman lost her child because of a drunk driver. She got so angry that she resolved that society should not tolerate this kind of irresponsible behavior. She organized people all over the United States to fight drunk driving. She and her association, with thousands of members, became a significant force and succeeded in their pursuit to change legislation in Congress and various state legislatures. That is an example of turning a negative emotion, like anger, into a strength by doing positive. She converted her anger into a resolution.

Have Patience

Patience creates confidence, decisiveness, and a rational outlook, which eventually leads to success.

— Brian Adams

A lot of times we hear people saying that one exposure to a positive or a negative material does not have any impact. That is not true. The difference may not be visible, but something is happening.

In China there is a bamboo tree that is planted, watered and fertilized for the first four years and nothing happens. There is no visible sign of growth. But sometime during the fifth year, the bamboo tree grows about

90 feet in six weeks. The question is: Did the bamboo tree grow in six weeks or did it take five years to grow? If the bamboo had not received water and fertilizer during the four years, when there was no visible sign of growth, would the plant had flourished? No. The bamboo tree would have died. The lesson is clear. Have patience and faith and keep doing the right thing. Even though the results may not be visible, something is happening.

Caution: We must distinguish between patience and laziness. Sometimes a person may be sheer lazy but they might think that they are being patient.

A good *beginning* makes a good ending.

— English proverb

Take Inventory: Make a List of All Your Strengths and Weaknesses

Successful people realize their limitations but build on their strengths. Unless we know these things, how can we build on them? Focus on what you want to do and be, rather than what you don't.

STRENGTHS	WEAKNESSES
_____	_____
_____	_____
_____	_____
_____	_____
_____	_____

The crux of self-esteem cannot be expressed better than in the following words by Abraham Lincoln.

WORLD, MY SON STARTS SCHOOL TODAY!*

World, take my child by the hand—he starts school today!

It is all going to be strange and new to him for a while, and I wish you would sort of treat him gently. You see, up to now, he has been king of the roost. He has been the boss of the backyard. I have always been around to repair his wounds, and I have always been handy to soothe his feelings.

But now things are going to be different. This morning he is going to walk down the front steps, wave his hand, and start on a great adventure that probably will include wars and tragedy and sorrow.

To live in this world will require faith and love and courage. So, World, I wish you would sort of take him by his young hand and teach him the things he will have to know. Teach him—but gently, if you can.

He will have to learn, I know, that all people are not just—that all men and women are not true. Teach him that for every scoundrel, there is a hero; that for every enemy, there is a friend. Let him learn early that the bullies are the easiest people to lick.

Teach him the wonder of books. Give him quiet time to ponder the eternal mystery of birds in the sky, bees in the sun, and flowers on a green hill. Teach him that it is far more honorable to fail than to cheat. Teach him to have faith in his own ideas, even if everyone tells him they are wrong.

---

*Adapted from "Pulpit Helps" February 1991, quoted in *Apple Seeds*, Volume 10, No. 1, 1994

Try to give my son the strength not to follow the crowd when everyone else is getting on the bandwagon. Teach him to listen to others, but to filter all he hears on a screen of truth and to take only the good that comes through.

Teach him never to put a price tag on his heart and soul. Teach him to close his ears on the howling mob— and to stand and fight if he thinks he is right. Teach him gently, World, but do not coddle him, because only the test of fire makes fine steel.

This is a big order, World, but see what you can do. He is such a nice son.

— Signed, Abraham Lincoln

ACTION PLAN

1. Read life stories of people who have turned negatives into positives. Make reading good books or listening to inspirational audio tapes part of your daily routine.
2. Regularly and systematically commit a portion of your time and/or money to charitable activity without any expectations in cash or kind.
3. Stay away from negative influences. Don't give in to peer pressure.
4. Practice giving and receiving sincere compliments graciously.
5. Start accepting responsibility for your behavior and actions.
6. Practice self-discipline even when it is not comfortable.
7. Associate with people of high moral character.
8. Be creative and find ways to turn your weaknesses into strengths.
9. Practice patience; persevere even if the results are not visible.

THE IMPORTANCE OF INTERPERSONAL SKILLS

Building a pleasing personality

I will pay more for the ability to deal with people than for any other ability under the sun.

—John D. Rockefeller

IN business, most problems are people problems. When we solve our people problems, our business problems are substantially resolved. People knowledge, is more important than product knowledge. Successful people build pleasing and magnetic personalities, which is what makes them charismatic. This helps in getting friendly cooperation from others.

A pleasing personality is easy to recognize but hard to define. It is apparent in the way a person walks and talks, his tone of voice, the warmth in his behavior and his definitive level of confidence. A pleasing personality is a combination of a person's attitude, behavior and expressions. You will never lose your attractiveness regardless of age when the path of your personality flows both from your face and your heart. Wearing a pleasant expression is more important than anything else you wear. It takes a lot more than a shoeshine and a manicure to give a person polish. Charming manners that disguise a poor character may work in the short run, but character reveals itself rather quickly. Relationships based on talent and personality alone, without character, make life miserable. Charisma without character is like good looks without goodness. The bottom line is, that a lasting, winning combination requires both character and charisma.

Be courteous to all, but intimate with a few, and let those few be well tried before you give them your confidence. True friendship is a plant of slow growth, and must undergo and withstand the shocks of adversity before it is entitled to the appellation.

— George Washington, January 15, 1783

LIFE IS AN ECHO

A little boy got angry with his mother and shouted at her, "I hate you, I hate you." Because of fear of reprimand, he ran out of the house. He went up to the valley and shouted, "I hate you, I hate you," and the echo returned, "I hate you, I hate you." Having never heard an echo before, he was scared, and ran to his mother for protection. He said there was a bad boy in the valley who shouted "I hate you, I hate you." The mother understood and she asked her son to go back and shout, "I love you, I love you." The little boy went and shouted, "I love you, I love you," and back came the echo. That taught the little boy a lesson—that our life is like an echo: We get back what we give.

LIFE IS A BOOMERANG

Benjamin Franklin said, "When you are good to others, you are best to yourself."

Whether it is your thoughts, actions or behavior, sooner or later they return—and with great accuracy.

Treat people with respect on your way up because you will be meeting them on your way down.

The following story is taken from *The Best of... Bits & Pieces.**

---

*Economic Press, Fairfield, NJ, 1994, pp. 84-85.

Many years ago two boys were working their way through Stanford University. Their funds got desperately low, and the idea came to them to engage Ignacy Paderewski for a piano recital. They would use the funds to help pay their board and tuition.

The great pianist's manager asked for a guarantee of $2,000. The guarantee was a lot of money in those days, but the boys agreed and proceeded to promote the concert. They worked hard, only to find that they had grossed only $1,600.

After the concert the two boys told the great artist the bad news. They gave him the entire $1,600, along with a promissory note for $400, explaining that they would earn the amount at the earliest possible moment and send the money to him. It looked like the end of their college careers.

"No, boys," replied Paderewski, that won't do." Then, tearing the note in two, he returned the money to them as well. "Now," he told them, "take out of this $1,600 all of your expenses and keep for each of you 10 percent of the balance for your work. Let me have the rest."

The years rolled by. World War I came and went. Paderewski, now premier of Poland, was striving to feed thousands of starving people in his native land. The only person in the world who could help him was Herbert Hoover, who was in charge of the US Food and Relief Bureau. Hoover responded and soon thousands of tons of food were sent to Poland.

After the starving people were fed, Paderewski journeyed to Paris to thank Hoover for the relief sent to him.

"That's all right, Mr. Paderewski," was Hoover's reply. "Besides, you don't remember it, but you helped me once when I was a student at college, and I was in trouble."

It is one of the most beautiful compensations of life that no man can sincerely try to help another without helping himself.

— Ralph Waldo Emerson

Goodness has a way of coming back; that is the nature of the beast. One doesn't have to do good with a desire to get back. It just happens automatically.

What are Some Factors That Prevent Building and Maintaining Positive Relationships?

Most of them are self-explanatory or elaborated on later in this chapter.

1. Selfishness
2. Lack of courtesy
3. Inconsiderate behavior
4. Not meeting commitments
5. Rude behavior
6. Lack of integrity and honesty
7. Self-centeredness
   (a person all wrapped up in himself makes a pretty small package)
8. Arrogance
   (an arrogant person is content with his opinion and knowledge. That will guarantee him perpetual ignorance).
9. Conceit
   (since nature abhors a vacuum, she fills empty heads with conceit)

John bragged, "My son got his intelligence from me." His wife replied, "I am sure he does, because I have still got mine."

- Negative attitude
- Closed mind
- Lack of listening
- Suspicious nature
- Lack of respect for values (low morals)

- Lack of discipline
- Lack of compassion (cruelty is a sign of weakness)
- Impatience
- Anger
  (temper gets a person in trouble and ego keeps him there).
- Manipulative behavior
- Escapist behavior
- Touchy nature
- Inconsistency
- Unwillingness to accept the truth
- Past bad experience
- An uncaring attitude
  (being ignored is not a good feeling; it shows a lack of concern).
- **Greed— is like sea water: the more you drink, the thirstier you get.**

This probably is not an all-inclusive list. Most of us may have some of the characteristics mentioned above. Some may have more of one than the other. The objective is to evaluate and adjust course in those areas.

THE DIFFERENCE BETWEEN EGO AND PRIDE

The biggest hurdle in building a positive relationship is Ego. Ego is self-intoxicating. Ego is an unhealthy pride that results in arrogance. Healthy pride is a feeling of the pleasure of accomplishment with humility. Ego gives a swollen head while pride gives a swollen heart. A big head gives a big headache whereas a big heart gives humility.

No matter what the size of a person's accomplishments are, there is never an excuse for having a big head. Pride, yes; big head, no.

Ego—The "I Know It All" Attitude

To an egocentric person, the world begins, ends and revolves around him. An egotist can be funny by default. A boss asked one of his employees how badly he wanted a raise. The employee said, "Real badly. I have been praying to God for one." The boss replied, "You are not going to get it because you went over my head." An egotist talks down to and looks down on others.

Egotism is the anesthetic that deadens the pain of stupidity.

— Knute Rockne

WHAT IS THE DIFFERENCE BETWEEN SELFISHNESS AND SELF-INTEREST?

It is important to understand the distinction between selfishness and self-interest.

Selfishness is negative and destructive. It destroys relationships because it is based on negative values. It believes in the win-lose principle. Self-interest is positive. It welcomes prosperity, peace of mind, good health and happiness. Self-interest believes in win-win situations.

Envy/Jealousy—Crab Mentality

Jealousy is ...a tiger that tears not only its prey but also its own raging heart.

— Michael Beer

What is crab mentality? Did you know that if you put a group of crabs in a box with an open top, that the crabs will stay in the box? The crabs could easily crawl out of the box and go free. But this doesn't happen, because the crab mentality doesn't let it happen. The moment one crab starts crawling up, the others pull it down and nobody gets out. They could all go free, but guess where they all end up? Dead.

The same thing is true with people who are jealous. They never get ahead in life and prevent others from succeeding. Jealousy is a sign of poor self-esteem. It is a universal trait. The biggest problem comes when jealousy becomes part of a nation's character. It results in disastrous consequences. Jealousy corrupts people and countries.

One Should Have an Open Mind Rather Than an Empty Mind

What is the difference between an open mind and an empty mind? An open mind is flexible; it evaluates and may accept or reject ideas and concepts based on merit.

An empty mind is a dumping ground for good and bad. It accepts without evaluation.

WE SEE THINGS NOT THE WAY *THEY* ARE BUT THE WAY *WE* ARE

According to a legend, a wise man was sitting outside his village when a traveler came up and asked, "I am looking to move from my present village—what kind of people live in this village?" The wise man asked, "What kind of people live in your village?" The man said, "They are mean, cruel, rude." The wise man replied, "The same kind of people live in this village too." After some time another traveler came by and asked the same question, and the wise man asked him, "What kind of people live in your village?" And the traveler replied, "The people are very kind, courteous, polite and good." The wise man said, "You will find the same kind of people here too."

Generally, we see the world not the way it is but the way we are. Most of the time, other people's behavior is a reaction to our own. If our motives are good, we assume the motives of others are good too. If our intentions are bad, we assume that the intentions of others are bad.

TRUST

All relationships are trust relationships. Relationships between employer and employee, parent and child, husband and wife, student and teacher, buyer and seller, and customer and salesperson are all trust relationships. How can we have trust without integrity? Crisis in trust really means crisis in truth. Trust results from being trustworthy.

What are the factors that build trust?

- Reliability—gives predictability and comes from commitment.
- Consistency—builds confidence.
- Respect—to self and others gives dignity and shows a caring attitude.
- Fairness—appeals to justice and integrity.
- Openness—shows a willingness to listen and share your views.
- Congruence—action and words harmonize. If a person says one thing and behaves differently, how

can you trust that person?

- Competence—comes when a person has the ability and the attitude to serve.
- Integrity—the key ingredient to trust.
- Acceptance—inspite of our effort to improve we need to accept each other with our pluses and minuses.
- Character—a person may have all the competence but if he lacks character he can't be trusted.
- Courage—a person who lacks courage will let you down in a crisis.

Trust in many ways is a much greater compliment than love. There are some people we love but we can't trust them. Relationships are like bank accounts: The more we deposit, the larger they become; therefore, the more we can draw from them. However, if you try to draw without depositing, it leads to disappointment.

Many times we feel we are overdrawn but, in reality, we may be under-deposited.

Below are some of the consequences of poor relationships and the lack of trust.

- Stress
- Lack of communication
- Irritation
- Closemindedness
- No team spirit
- Lack of credibility
- Poor self-esteem
- Suspicion
- Loss of productivity
- Isolation
- Poor health
- Distrust
- Anger
- Prejudice
- Breakdown of morale
- Uncooperative behavior
- Conflict
- Frustration
- Unhappiness

ACTION PLAN

1. Take a few moments to assess the messages you are sending out. Do you send positive or negative messages? If it's the latter, make a concerted effort to change your messages. Start looking for the good it will be there for you to find.

2. Go over the following list of factors that prevent building and maintaining positive relationships. If you find yourself in possession of any of these traits, pick one a week to work on eliminating them.
   - Selfishness
   - Lack of courtesy
   - Inconsiderate behavior
   - Not meeting commitments
   - Rude behavior
   - Lack of integrity and honesty
   - Self-centeredness
   - Arrogance
   - Conceit

8

25 STEPS TO BUILDING A POSITIVE PERSONALITY

He who would learn to fly one day must first learn to stand and walk and run...

— Friederich Nietzsche

Step 1: Accept Responsibility

"Responsibilities gravitate to the person who can shoulder them."

— Elbert Hubbard

WHEN people accept additional responsibility they are actually giving themselves a promotion.

Responsible behavior is to accept accountability. That represents maturity. Acceptance of responsibility is a reflection of our attitude and the environment we operate in. Most people are quick to take credit for what goes right but very few would readily accept responsibility when things go wrong. A person who does not accept responsibility is not absolved from being responsible. Your objective is to cultivate responsible behavior.

Stop the Blame Game

Avoid phrases such as:

- everyone else does it,
- or no one does it, or
- it is all your fault.

People who don't accept responsibility shift the blame to their parents, teachers and genes. God, fate, luck or the stars. Responsible behavior should be inculcated right from childhood. It cannot be taught without a certain degree of obedience.

Johnny said, "Mama, Jimmy broke the window." Mama asked, "How did he do it?" Johnny replied, "I threw a stone at him and he ducked."

People who use their privileges without accepting responsibility usually end up losing their privileges.

Responsibility involves thoughtful action.

Pettiness Causes Us to Ignore Our Responsibilities

Think about it. Petty minds are busy passing the buck rather than doing what needs to be done.

Social Responsibility

Ancient Indian wisdom teaches us that our first responsibility is to the community, second to our family and third to ourselves. When this hierarchy is reversed, a society starts degenerating. Social responsibility ought to be the moral obligation of every citizen. Responsibility and freedom go hand in hand. A sign of a good citizen is that he is willing to pull his own weight.

The price of greatness is responsibility.

— Winston Churchill

Societies are not destroyed so much by the activities of rascals but by the inactivity of the good people. What a paradox! If good people can tolerate destruction by being inactive, how can they be good? The question is, are they discharging their social responsibility?

For evil to flourish, good people have to do nothing and evil shall flourish.

— Edmund Burke

Step 2: Show Consideration

A ten-year-old boy went to an ice-cream shop, sat at a table, and asked the waitress, "How much is an ice-cream cone?" She said, "seventy-five cents." The boy started counting the coins he had in his hand. Then he asked how much a small cup of ice-cream was. The waitress impatiently replied, "sixty-five cents." The boy said, "I will have the small ice-cream cup." The boy ate his ice-cream, paid the bill, and left. When the waitress came to pick up the empty plate, she was touched. Underneath were ten one-cent coins left as the tip. The young boy had consideration for the waitress before he ordered his ice-cream. He showed sensitivity and caring. He thought of others before himself.

If we all thought like the little boy, we would have a great place to live. Show consideration, courtesy and politeness. Thoughtfulness shows a caring attitude.

Step 3: Think Win-Win

A man died and St. Peter asked him if he would like to go to heaven or hell. The man asked if he could see both before deciding. St. Peter took him to hell first. There the man saw a big hall containing a long table, laden with many kinds of food. He also saw rows of people with pale, sad faces. They looked starved and there was no laughter. And he observed one more thing: Their hands were tied to four-foot forks and knives and they were trying to get the food from the center of the table to put into their mouths. But they couldn't.

Then, St. Peter took him to see heaven. There he saw a big hall with a long table, with lots of food. He noticed rows of people on both sides of the table with their hands tied to four-foot forks and knives also. But here people were laughing and were well fed and healthy-looking. The people were feeding one another across the table. The result was happiness, prosperity, enjoyment and gratification because they were not thinking of themselves alone; they were thinking win-win. The same is true of our lives. When we serve our customers, our families, our employers and employees, we automatically win.

Step 4: Choose Your Words Carefully

A person who says what ever he likes usually ends up hearing what he doesn't like. Be tactful. Tact consists of choosing one's words carefully and knowing how far to go. It also means knowing what to say and what to leave unsaid. Talent without tact may not always be desirable. Words reflect attitude. Words can hurt feelings and destroy relationships. More people have been hurt by an improper choice of words than by any natural disaster. Choose what you say rather than say what you choose. That is the difference between wisdom and foolishness.

Excessive talking does not mean communication. Talk less; say more.

A fool speaks without thinking; a wise man thinks before speaking.

Words spoken out of bitterness can cause irreparable damage. The way parents speak to their children in many instances shapes their children's destiny.

SPOKEN WORDS CAN'T BE RETRIEVED

A farmer slandered his neighbor. Realizing his mistake, he went to the preacher to ask for forgiveness. The preacher told him to take a bag of feathers and drop them in the center of town. The farmer did as he was told. Then the preacher asked him to go and collect the feathers and put them back in the bag. The farmer tried but couldn't as the feathers had all blown away. When he returned with the empty bag, the preacher said, "The same thing is true about your words. You dropped them rather easily but you cannot retrieve them. You need to be very careful in choosing your words."

Step 5: Don't Criticize and Complain

When I talk of criticism, I refer to negative criticism. When a person is criticized, he becomes defensive. A critic is often like a back-seat driver who drives the driver mad. Does that mean we should never criticize, nor can we give positive criticism?

Positive Criticism

How do you offer constructive criticism? Criticize with a spirit of helpfulness rather than as a put-down. Offer solutions in your criticism. Criticize the behavior not the person, because when we criticize the person, we hurt their self-esteem. The right to criticize comes with the desire to help. As long as the act of criticizing does not give pleasure to the giver, it is okay. When giving criticism becomes a pleasure, it is time to stop.

Some suggestions for giving criticism that motivates others:

- Be a coach—criticize with a helpful attitude. A coach criticizes to help improve performance of the athlete.
- Understanding and concern will act as a motivator.
- The attitude should be corrective rather than punitive.
- Be specific, rather than saying things like "you *always*" or "you *never*." Vague criticism causes resentment.
- Get your facts right. Don't jump to conclusions. We all have the right to our opinions but we don't have

the right to incorrect facts. Don't rush to criticize.
- Maintain your cool but be firm.
- Criticize to persuade, not intimidate.
- Don't be sarcastic as it builds resentment.
- If criticism is given appropriately, it will reduce the need for repetition.
- Criticize in private not in public. Why? Because it maintains goodwill whereas public criticism can be humiliating.
- Give the other person an opportunity to explain his side.
- Show them how they would benefit from correcting their mistake.
- Point out the loss from not correcting it.
- Rather than telling ask for suggestions for improvement.
- Question the action, not the intent. If intent is in question, then it is better to terminate the relationship.
- Criticize the performance, not the performer.
- Don't express personal resentment.
- Keep criticism in perspective. Don't overdo it. Criticism is like giving medication. The medication should be the right mixture with a perfect dosage. Too much will have adverse effects and too little will be ineffective. Given in a positive way in the right dosage, it can work wonders.
- When someone realizes and admits his mistake and apologizes. Let him save face.
- Close on a positive note with appreciation.

Receiving Criticism

There will be times when you will be criticized, sometimes justly and sometimes unjustly. The greatest people in the world have been criticized. Justified criticism can be very helpful and should be taken positively as feedback. Unjustified criticism is really a compliment in disguise. It is the average person who hates winners. When people are not successful and have nothing else to talk about they make you the target.

The only way you will never be criticized is if you do nothing, say nothing or have nothing. You will end up being a big nothing.

Unjust criticism comes from two sources:

1. Ignorance. When criticism is given out of ignorance, it can easily be eliminated or corrected by building awareness of the facts.
2. Jealousy. When criticism springs from jealousy, take it as a compliment in disguise. You are being unjustly criticized because the other person wants to be where you are. The tree that bears the most fruits also gets the most stones.

There is another breed of people who are willing to help others until the others are able to help themselves. But as soon as they are able to help themselves, this group of people make life as miserable and as uncomfortable as possible. This is part of life and if we have to succeed, we have to do it in spite of them. This kind of behavior is the result of jealousy.

An inability to accept constructive criticism is a sign of poor self-esteem. Suggestions for accepting criticism:

- Take it in the right spirit. Deal with it graciously rather than grudgingly.
- Evaluate it with an open mind, if it makes sense accept it, learn from it and implement it.
- Don't be defensive. Accept constructive criticism immediately and emphatically. Why? Because it disarms the other person. If we don't it will irritate

him even more and in future he will not give constructive criticism. If we use this as a tactic if will
only work once, but if we are sincere it will work
time after time.
- Thank the person who gives constructive criticism
because he means well and has helped you.
- A person with high self-esteem accepts positive
criticism and becomes better, not bitter.

The problem with most people is they would rather
be ruined by false praise than culprit by constructive
criticism.

Complaints

Some people are chronic complainers. If it is hot, it is
too hot. If it is cold, it is too cold. Every day is a bad
day. They complain even if everything goes right. Why
complain? Because 50% of the people don't care if you
have got a problem and the other 50% are happy that
you have got a problem. What is the point of complaining? Nothing comes out of it. It becomes a
personality trait. Does that mean we should never
complain or invite complaints? Not at all. Just like
criticism, if it is done in a positive way, complaints can
be very useful. A constructive complaint:
  (a) shows that the complainer cares.
  (b) gives the receiver of complaints a second chance
      to correct himself.

Step 6: Smile and Be Kind

SMILE*

A smile costs nothing, but it creates much.

---

*Adapted from *The Best of ... Bits & Pieces*, Economic Press, Fairfield, NJ, 1994,
p. 170.

It enriches those who receive it without impoverishing those who give it.
It happens in a flash, and the memory of it may last forever. None are so rich that they can get along without it, and none so poor that they cannot be richer for its benefits.
It creates happiness in the home, fosters goodwill in a business, and is the countersign of friends.
It is rest to the weary, daylight to the discouraged, sunshine to the sad, and nature's best antidote for trouble.
Yet it cannot be begged, bought, borrowed, or stolen, for it is something that is worth nothing to anyone until it is given away.
In the course of the day, some of your acquaintances may be too tired to give you a smile. Give them one of yours. Nobody needs a smile so much as those who have none left to give.

Cheerfulness flows from goodness. A smile can be fake or genuine. The key is to have a genuine one. It takes more muscles to frown than to smile. It is easier to smile than frown. It improves face value. Who likes to be around a grouch? No one except may be a bigger grouch! A smile is contagious and is an inexpensive way to improve looks. A smiling face is always welcome.

Step 7: Put Positive Interpretation on Other People's Behavior

In the absence of sufficient facts, people instinctively put a negative interpretation on others' actions or inactions. Some people suffer from "paranoia": they think the world is out to get them. That is not true. By starting with positive assumptions, we have a better chance of building a pleasing personality resulting, in good relationships.

For example, how often have we put through a call and not gotten a reply from the other party for two days and the first thought that comes to our mind is, "They never cared to return my call" or "They ignored me." That is negative. Maybe:

- they tried, but couldn't get through
- they left a message we didn't get
- they had an emergency
- they never got the message.

There could be many reasons. It is worth giving the benefit of doubt to the other person and starting on a positive note.

Step 8: Be a Good Listener

One often reads that the art of conversation is dying. But wouldn't you agree that infinitely more valuable and rare is a good listener.

Ask yourself these questions. How does it make you feel when you wanted somebody to listen to you and

- They did more talking than listening?
- They disagreed with the first thing you said.
- They interrupted you at every step.
- They were impatient and completed every sentence you started.
- They were physically present but mentally absent.
- They heard but didn't listen. You had to repeat the same thing three times because the other person wasn't listening.
- They came to conclusions unrelated to facts.
- They asked questions on unrelated topics.
- They were fidgety and distracted.
- They were obviously not listening or paying attention.

All these things show disinterest in the person or the topic and a total lack of courtesy.

Do the following words describe the feeling of not being listened to?

- Neglected
- Rejected
- Dejected
- Let down
- Unimportant
- Small
- Ignored
- Belittled
- Annoyed
- Stupid
- Worthless
- Embarrassed
- Demotivated
- Disheartened

Let's reverse the scenario. How does it make you feel when you want someone to listen to you and they

- make you comfortable.
- give you their undivided attention.
- ask appropriate and relevant questions.
- show interest in your subject.

Do the following words describe the feeling of being listened to?

- Important
- Pleased
- Satisfied
- Worthwhile
- Cared for
- Good
- Happy
- Appreciated
- Encouraged
- Inspired

What are some of the barriers to effective listening?

External Barriers	*Internal Barriers*
physical	distractions preoccupation or absent-mindedness
noise	prejudice and prejudging people
fatigue	no interest in subject or speaker

There could be intellectual barriers, such as language, comprehension, etc. In order to inspire others to speak, be a good listener.

Listening shows caring. When you show a caring attitude toward another person, that person feels important. When he feels important, what happens? He is more motivated and more receptive to your ideas.

An open ear is the only believable sign of an open heart.

—David Augsburger

In order to be a good listener:

- Encourage the speaker to talk.
- Ask questions. It shows interest.
- Don't interrupt.
- Don't change the topic.
- Show understanding and respect.
- Pay attention, concentrate.
- Avoid distractions.
- Show empathy.
- Be open-minded. Don't let preconceived ideas and prejudices prevent you from listening.
- Concentrate on the message and not on the delivery.
- Recognize the nonverbal communication, such as facial expressions, eye contact, etc. They might be communicating a different message from the verbal.
- Listen to feelings and not just words.

Step 9: Be Enthusiastic

Nothing great is ever achieved without enthusiasm.

—Ralph Waldo Emerson

Enthusiasm and success go hand in hand, but enthusiasm comes first. Enthusiasm inspires confidence, raises morale, builds loyalty and is priceless. Enthusiasm is contagious. You can feel enthusiasm by the way a person talks, walks or shakes hands. Enthusiasm is a habit that one can acquire and practice.

Many decades ago, Charles Schwab, who was earning a salary of a million dollars a year, was asked if he was being paid such a high salary because of his exceptional ability to produce steel. Charles Schwab replied, "I consider my ability to arouse enthusiasm among the men the greatest asset I possess, and the way to develop the best that is in a man is by appreciation and encouragement."

Live while you are alive. Don't die before you are dead. Enthusiasm and desire are what change mediocrity to excellence. Water turns into steam with a difference of only one degree in temperature and steam can move some of the biggest engines in the world. That is what enthusiasm helps us to do in our lives.

Step 10: Give Honest and Sincere Appreciation

The psychologist William James said, "One of the deepest desires of human beings is the desire to be appreciated. The feeling of being unwanted is hurtful."

Expensive jewels are not real gifts; they are apologies for shortcomings. Many times we buy gifts for people to compensate for not spending enough time with them. Real gifts are when you give a part of yourself.

Sincere appreciation is one of the greatest gifts one can give to another person. It makes a person feel important. The desire to feel important is one of the greatest cravings in most human beings. It can be a great motivator.

The biggest disease today is not leprosy or tuberculosis but rather the feeling of being unwanted.

— Mother Teresa

In order to be effective, appreciation must meet certain criteria:

1. It must be *specific.* If I tell someone that he did a good job, and walk away, what will go through his mind? He will think, "What did I do good?" He will be confused. But when I say, "The way you handled that difficult customer was great," then he knows what he is being appreciated for.
2. It must be *immediate.* The effectiveness is diluted if we show our appreciation for someone six months after he has done something commendable.
3. It must be *sincere.* It must come from the heart. You must mean every word. It is better not to appreciate if you don't mean it because insincerity comes through.
4. Don't qualify praise with a *but.* By using the but as a connector, we erase the appreciation. Use "and," "in addition to that" or some other appropriate connector. Instead of saying, "I appreciate your effort but....", say something like, "I appreciate your effort and would you please...."
5. After giving appreciation, it is not important to wait for a receipt or acknowledgment. Some people are looking for a compliment in return. That is not the purpose of appreciation.

If you are receiving appreciation, accept it graciously with a "thank-you."

It is easier to deal with honest rejection than insincere appreciation. At least the person knows where he stands. Don't miss out any opportunity to give sincere appreciation. It builds the other person's self-esteem and automatically your own self-esteem goes up. Public appreciation is recognition.

Caution: Without clear benchmarks appreciation may cause resentment.

What is the difference between appreciation and flattery?

The difference is sincerity. One comes from the heart, the other from the mouth. One is sincere and the other has an ulterior motive. Some people find it easier to flatter than to give sincere praise. Don't flatter or get taken in by flatterers.

> *It's an old maxim in the schools*
> *that flattery's the food of fools*
> *Yet now and then you men of wit*
> *will condescend to take a bit.*
>
> — Jonathan Swift

Insincere appreciation is like a mirage in the desert. The closer you get, the more disappointed you become because it is nothing more than an illusion. People put up a front of sincerity as a cover up.

Step 11: When You Make a Mistake, Accept It And Move On

"When I am wrong, make me easy to change; and when I am right, make me easy to live with." This is a good philosophy to live by.

Some people live and learn while others live and never learn. Mistakes are to be learned from. The greatest mistake a person can make is to repeat it. Don't assign blame and make excuses. Don't dwell on it. When you realize your mistake, it is a good idea to accept responsibility for it and apologize. Don't defend it. Why? Acceptance disarms the other person.

Step 12: Discuss But Don't Argue

Arguments can be avoided and a lot of heartache prevented by being a little careful. The best way to win an argument is to avoid it. An argument is one thing you will never win. If you win, you lose; if you lose, you lose. If you win an argument but lose a good job, customer, friend or marriage, what kind of victory is it? Pretty empty. Arguments result from inflated ego.

Arguing is like fighting a losing battle. Even if one wins, the cost may be more than the victory is worth. Emotional battles leave a residual ill will even if you win.

In an argument, both people are trying to have the last word. Argument is nothing more than a battle of egos and results in a yelling contest. A bigger fool than the one who knows it all is the one who argues with him!

Is It Worth It?

The more arguments you win, the fewer friends you have. Even if you are right, is it worth arguing? The answer is pretty obvious. A big no. Does that mean one should never bring up a point that contradicts another? One should, but gently and tactfully, by saying something neutral such as "based on my information..." If the other person is argumentative, even if you can prove him wrong, is it worth it? I don't think so. Do you make your point a second time? I wouldn't. Why? Because the argument is coming from a closed mind trying to prove who is right rather than what is right.

For example, at a social get-together, especially after a few drinks, someone may say authoritatively, "The current year's export figures are $50 billion." You happen to know that his information is incorrect and the right figure is $45 billion. You read it in the paper that morning, or you heard it on the radio on the way to the get-together and you have a bulletin in your car to substantiate it. Do you make your point? Yes, by saying, "My information is that the export figure is $45 billion." The other person reacts, "You don't know what you are talking about. I know exactly what it is and it is $50 billion."

At this point, you have several choices:

1. Make your point again and start an argument.
2. Run and bring the bulletin from your car and make sure you prove him wrong.
3. Discuss but don't argue.
4. Avoid it.

The right choices are numbers 3 and 4.

If one wants to accomplish great things in life one has to practice maturity. Maturity means not getting entangled in unimportant things and petty arguments.

What is the Difference Between an Argument and a Discussion?

- An argument throws heat; a discussion throws light.
- One stems from ego and a closed mind whereas the other comes from an open mind.

- An argument is an exchange of ignorance whereas a discussion is an exchange of knowledge.
- An argument is an expression of temper whereas a discussion is an expression of logic.
- An argument tries to prove who is right whereas a discussion tries to prove what is right.

It is not worthwhile to reason with a prejudiced mind; it wasn't reasoned into him so you can't reason it out. A narrow mind and a big mouth usually lead to pointless arguments.

In order to discuss, let the other person state his side of the case without interruption. Let him blow steam. Don't try to prove him wrong on every point. Never let him drag you to his level. Treat him with courtesy and respect; that will confuse him.

Regardless of the cause, the best way to diffuse the situation is to:

1. give a patient hearing.
2. not fight back or retaliate—that will confuse the other person because he was expecting a fight.
3. not expect an apology. For some people, apologizing is difficult even if they have made a mistake.
4. not make issues out of petty matters.

Discussion entails not only saying the right thing at the right time but also leaving unsaid what need not be said.

Children should be taught the art of speaking up but not talking back. As adults we should learn the art of disagreeing without being disagreeable.

The way a person handles an argument reflects their upbringing.

I learned a long time ago never to wrestle with a pig. You get dirty and besides, the pig likes it.

—Cyrus Ching

Steps to Opening a Discussion

1. Be open-minded.
2. Don't be dragged into an argument.
3. Don't interrupt.
4. Listen to the other person's point of view before giving your own.
5. Ask questions to clarify. That will also set the other person thinking.
6. Don't exaggerate.
7. Be enthusiastic in convincing, not forceful.
8. Be willing to yield.
9. Be flexible on petty things but not on principles.
10. Don't make it a prestige issue.
11. Give your opponent a graceful way to withdraw without hurting his pride. Rejection can be hurtful.
12. Use soft words but hard arguments rather than hard words and soft arguments.

It is impossible to defeat an ignorant man in an argument. His strong and bitter words only indicate a weak cause.

During a discussion, it may be a good idea to use phrases such as:

- It appears to me ...
- I may be wrong ...

Another way to defuse arguments is by showing ignorance and asking questions such as:

- Why do you feel that way?
- Can you explain a little?
- Can you be more specific?

If nothing works, it may be worthwhile to politely, gently and with courtesy, agree to disagree.

Step 13: Don't Gossip

Remember, people who gossip with you will also gossip about you in your absence.

Gossiping and lying are closely related. A gossip listens in haste and repeats at leisure. A gossip never minds his own business because he has neither a mind nor a business. A gossip is more concerned about what he overhears than what he hears. Gossip is the art of saying nothing in a way that leaves nothing unsaid.

Someone said it well: "Small people talk about other people, mediocre people talk about things, great people talk about ideas."

Gossip can lead to slander and defamation of character. People who listen to gossip are as guilty as those who do the gossiping.

A gossip usually gets caught in his own mouth trap. Gossip has no respect for justice. It breaks hearts, it ruins lives, it is cunning and malicious. It victimizes the helpless. Gossip is hard to track down because it has no face or name. It tarnishes reputations, topples governments, wrecks marriages, ruins careers, makes the innocent cry, causes heartaches and sleepless nights. The next time you indulge in gossip, ask yourself.

- Is it the truth?
- Is it kind and gentle?
- Is it necessary?
- Am I spreading rumors?
- Do I say positive things about others?
- Do I enjoy and encourage others to spread rumors?
- Does my conversation begin with, "Don't tell anyone?"
- Can I maintain confidentiality?

Refrain from indulging in gossip. Remember, small talk comes out of big mouths.

Step 14: Turn Your Promises into Commitments

What is the difference between a promise and a commitment? A promise is a statement of intent. A commitment is a promise that is going to be kept no matter what. In the no matter what, I exclude illegal and immoral things. Commitment comes out of character and leads to conviction.

Can you imagine what kind of a world it would be if people didn't keep their commitments? What would happen to relationships between

- spouses?
- employers and employees?
- parents and children?
- students and teachers?
- buyers and sellers?

Uncommitted relationships are shallow and hollow. They are a matter of convenience and are temporary. Nothing lasting has ever been created without commitment.

Commitment says, "I am predictable in the unpredictable future."

Many people confuse commitment with confinement. That really is not true. Commitment does not take away freedom; it actually gives more freedom because it provides a sense of security.

The most important commitment we ever make is to your values. That is why it is imperative to have good value system. For example, if I committed myself to support a leader who later becomes a drug dealer, do I continue my commitment? Not at all.

Commitment leads to enduring relationships through thick and thin. It shows in a person's personality and relationships.

Step 15: Be Grateful But Do Not Expect Gratitude

Gratitude is a beautiful word. Gratitude is a feeling. It improves our personality and builds character. Gratitude develops out of humility. It is a feeling of thankfulness towards others. It is conveyed through our attitude towards others and reflects in our behavior. Gratitude does not mean reciprocating good deeds gratitude is not give and take. Kindness, understanding and patience cannot be repaid. What does gratitude teach us? It teaches us the art of cooperation and understanding. Gratitude must be sincere. A simple thank you can be gracious. Many times we forget to be thankful to the people closest to us, such as our spouse, our relatives, our friends. Gratitude would rank among the top qualities that form the character and personality of an individual with integrity. Ego stands in the way of showing gratitude. A gracious attitude changes our outlook in life. With gratitude and humility, right actions come naturally.

Gratitude ought to be a way of life, something that we cannot give enough of. It can mean a smile, or a thank you, or a gesture of appreciation.

Think of your most precious possessions. What makes them special? In most cases, the gift is less significant than the giver. Seldom are we grateful for the things we already possess.

Think back and try to recall the people who had a positive influence on your life. Your parents, teachers, anyone who spent extra time to help you. Perhaps it appears that they just did their job. Not really. They willingly sacrificed their time, effort, money and many other things for you. They did it out of love and not for your thankfulness. At some point, a person realizes the effort that went in to help them shape their future. Perhaps it is not too late to thank them.

The Story of Christ

As the story goes, Christ healed ten lepers and when he turned back they were all gone except one who had the courtesy to thank him. Christ said, " I didn't do a thing." What is the moral of the story?

1. Human beings are ungrateful.
2 A grateful person is the exceptional person.
3. Christ literally gave them a new life and said, "I didn't do a thing."
4. Like Christ we should not expect gratitude.

How does this translate in our behavior and personality? We feed or give shelter to someone for a few days and say "Look what I did for the other person." We blow our giving out of proportion in our own mind. It is not uncommon to hear people saying, "If it wasn't for me, this person would be on the street." What an ego!

By the Way

When people ask others to do something for them by using the phrase "By the way, can you do this for me?" they undermine the importance of doing or not doing. I have found that if we have to do anything for anyone it is never "by the way," it is always "out of the way."

This does not amount to doing favors from the doer's perspective. If one doesn't do things that can be done to help another person, then it is sad. But I am convinced that there is no such thing as "By the way," it is always "out of the way" and it is *worth it.*

Step 16: Be Dependable and Practice Loyalty

The old adage, "an ounce of loyalty is worth more than a pound of cleverness," is universal and eternal.

Ability is important but dependability is crucial. If you have someone with all the ability but if he is not dependable, do you want him as part of your team? No, not at all.

I KNEW YOU WOULD COME

There were two childhood buddies who went through school and college and even joined the army together. War broke out and they were fighting in the same unit. One night they were ambushed. Bullets were flying all over and out of the darkness came a voice, "Harry, please come and help me." Harry immediately recognized the voice of his childhood buddy, Bill. He asked the captain if he could go. The captain said, "No, I can't let you go, I am already short-handed and I cannot afford to lose one more person. Besides, the way Bill sounds he is not going to make it." Harry kept quiet. Again the voice came, "Harry, please come and help me." Harry, sat quietly because the captain had refused earlier. Again and again the voice came. Harry couldn't contain himself any longer and told the captain, "Captain, this is my childhood buddy. I have to go and help." The captain reluctantly let him go. Harry crawled through the darkness and dragged Bill back into the trench. They found that Bill was dead. Now the captain got angry and shouted at Harry, "Didn't I tell you he was not going to make it? He is dead, you could have been killed and I could have become short handed. You made a mistake." Harry replied, "Captain, I did the right thing. When I reached Bill he was still alive and his last words were 'Harry, I knew you would come.'"

Good relationships are hard to find and once developed should be nurtured.

We are often told: Live your dream. But you cannot live your dream at the expense of others. People who do so are unscrupulous. We need to make personal sacrifices for our family, friends, those we care about and who depend on us.

Step 17: Avoid Bearing Grudges

Don't be a garbage collector. Have you heard the phrase I can forgive but I can't forget?

When a person refuses to forgive, he is locking doors that some day he might need to open. When we hold grudges and harbor resentments, who are we hurting the most? Ourselves.

 Jim and Jerry had been childhood friends but for whatever reasons, the relationship fell apart and they hadn't spoken for 25 years. Jerry was on his deathbed and didn't want to enter eternity with a heavy heart. So he called Jim, apologized and said, "Let's forgive each other and be done for the past." Jim thought it was a good idea and went to visit Jerry at the hospital.

They spent a couple of hours together catching up on the last 25 years—and patching up their differences. As Jim was leaving, Jerry shouted from behind, "Jim, just in case I don't die; remember, this forgiveness doesn't count." Life is too short to hold grudges. It is not worth it.

Shame on Me

While it is not worth holding grudges, it doesn't make sense to be bitten time and again. It is well said, "Cheat me once, shame on you; you cheat me twice, shame on me."

John Kennedy once said, *"Forgive the other person but don't forget their name."* I am sure that his message was that one should not get cheated twice.

Step 18: Practice Honesty, Integrity and Sincerity

Honesty means to be genuine and real versus fake and fictitious.

Build a reputation of being trustworthy. If there is one thing that builds any kind of relationship at home, at work, or socially, it is integrity.

Not keeping commitments amounts to dishonest behavior.

Honesty inspires openness, reliability and frankness. It shows respect for one's self and others. Honesty is in being, not in appearing to be. Lies may have speed but truth has endurance. Integrity is not found in company brochures or titles but in a person's character.

Is it worth compromising one's integrity and taking shortcuts to win? A person may win a trophy but knowing the truth, can never be a happy person. More important than winning a trophy is being a good human being.

A POUND OF BUTTER

There was a farmer who sold a pound of butter to a baker. One day the baker decided to weigh the butter to see if he was getting a pound and found that he was not. This angered him and he took the farmer to court. The judge asked the farmer how he was measuring the butter he was selling. The farmer replied, "Your Honor, I am primitive. I don't have a proper measure, but I do have a scale." The judge asked, 'Then how do you weigh the butter?" The farmer replied "Your Honor, long before the baker started buying butter from me, I have been buying a pound loaf of bread from him. Every day when the baker brings the bread, I put it on the scale and give him the same weight in butter. If anyone is to be blamed, it is the baker." We get back in life what we give to others.

Whenever you take an action, ask yourself: Am I giving fair value for the wages or money I hope to make?

Honesty and dishonesty becomes a habit. Some people practice dishonesty and can lie with a straight face. Others lie so much that they no longer know what the truth is. But whom are they deceiving? Themselves—more than anyone else.

Honesty can be put across gently. Some people take pride in being brutally honest. It seems they are getting a bigger kick out of the brutality than the honesty. Choice of words and tact are important.

Truth May Not Always Be What You Want to Hear

One can be truthful without being cruel but that may not always be the case. The most important responsibility of an honest friend is to be truthful. Some people, in order to avoid confronting painful truths, select friends who tell them what they want to hear. They kid themselves despite the fact that deep down they know they are not being truthful. Honest criticism can be painful. If you have many acquaintances and few friends, it is time to step back and explore the depth of your relationships.

A lack of honesty is sometimes labeled as tact, public relations or politics. But is it really so?

The problem with lying is that one has to remember one's lies.

Honesty requires firmness and commitment. How many times have we all been guilty of:

- little white lies?
- flattery?
- omitting facts or giving half-truths?
- telling the greatest lies by remaining silent?

Make yourself an honest man and then you may be sure there is one rascal less in the world.

— Thomas Carlyle

Credibility

We all know the story of the shepherd boy who cried wolf. The boy decided to have some fun at the expense of the villagers. He shouted, "Help, help, the wolf is here." The villagers heard him and came to his rescue. But when they got there, they saw no wolf and the boy laughed at them. They went away. The next day, the boy played the same trick and the same thing happened.

Then one day, while the boy was taking care of his sheep he actually saw a wolf and shouted for help. The people in the village heard him but this time nobody came to his rescue. They thought it was another trick and didn't trust him anymore. He lost his sheep to the wolf.

The moral of the story is

- When you tell lies, you lose credibility.
- Once you have lost credibility, even when you tell the truth, no one believes you.

The Quality of a Good Character is Honesty

Truth can be misrepresented in two ways:

1. Incomplete facts or information
2. Exaggeration

BEWARE OF HALF-TRUTHS OR MISREPRESENTATION OF TRUTHS

There was a sailor who worked on the same boat for three years. One night he got drunk. This was the first time it had ever happened. The captain recorded it in the log, "The sailor was drunk tonight." The sailor read it, and he knew this comment would affect his career, so he went to the captain, apologized and asked the captain to add that it only happened once in three years because that was the complete truth. The captain refused and said, "What I have written in the log is the truth."

The next day it was the sailor's turn to fill in the log. He wrote, "The captain was sober tonight." The captain read the comment and asked the sailor to change or add to it explaining the complete truth because this implied that the captain was drunk every other night. The sailor told the captain that what he had written in the log was the truth.

Both statements were true but they conveyed misleading messages.

Exaggeration

Exaggeration does two things:

1. It weakens our case and makes us lose credibility.
2. It is like an addiction. It becomes a habit. Some people can't tell the truth without exaggerating.

Be Sincere

Sincerity is a matter of intent and hard to prove. We can

achieve our goals by having a sincere desire to help others.

Stay Away from Pretense

Asking a friend in trouble, "Is there anything I can do for you," is really annoying. It is more lip service than a sincere offer. If you really want to help, think of something appropriate to be done and then do it.

Many people put on the cloak of sincerity more out of selfishness than substance, hoping that some day they could claim the right to receive help.

Stay away from meaningless and phony pleasantries.

Caution—sincerity is no measure of good judgment. Someone could be sincere, yet wrong.

ACTIONS SPEAK LOUDER THAN WORDS

WHICH LOVED BEST?

"I love you. Mother," said little John;
Then, forgetting his work, his cap went on,
And he was off to the garden swing,
And left her the water and wood to bring.
"I love you. Mother," said rosy Nell—
"I love you better than tongue can tell";
Then she teased and pouted full half the day,
Till her mother rejoiced when she went to play.
"I love you, Mother," said little Fan;
"Today I'll help you all I can;
How glad I am that school doesn't keep!"
So she rocked the babe till it fell asleep.
Then, stepping softly, she fetched the broom,
And swept the floor and tidied the room;

Busy and happy all day was she,
Helpful and happy as child could be.
"I love you, Mother," again they said,
Three little children going to bed;
How do you think that mother guessed
Which of them really loved her best?

—Joy Allison*

Maintain Integrity

Ancient wisdom says, "Anything that is bought or sold has no value unless it contains the secret, priceless ingredient—that, what cannot be traded." What is it? The secret, priceless ingredient of every product is the credibility, the honor and integrity of the one who makes it. It is not so secret but it is priceless.

Here is Another Side to Integrity—Questionable

Three executives were fighting over who would pay the bill for lunch. One said, "I will pay, I can get a tax deduction." The other said, "Let me have it, I will get reimbursement from my company." The third said, "Let me pay, because I am filing for bankruptcy next week."

Step 19: Practice Humility

Confidence without humility is arrogance. Humility is the foundation of all virtues. It is a sign of greatness. Humility does not mean self-demeaning behavior that would amount to belittling oneself. Sincere humility attracts but false humility detracts.

---

*In *The Book of Virtues,* edited by William J. Bennett, Simon & Schuster, New York, 1993, p. 204.

 Many years ago, a rider came across some soldiers who were trying to move a heavy log without success. The corporal was standing by as the men struggled. The rider asked the corporal why he wasn't helping. The corporal replied, "I am the corporal; I give orders." The rider dismounted, went up to the soldiers and helped them lift the log. With his help, the log got moved. The rider quietly mounted his horse and went to the corporal and said, "The next time your men need help, send for the Commander-in-Chief." After he left, the corporal and his men found out that the rider was George Washington.

The message is clear. Success and humility go hand in hand. When others blow your horn, the sound goes further. Just think about it? Simplicity and humility are two hallmarks of greatness.

Step 20: Be Understanding and Caring

In relationships we all make mistakes and sometimes we are insensitive to the needs of others, especially those very close to us. All this leads to disappointment and resentment. The answer to handling disappointment is understanding.

Relationships don't come about because people are perfect. They come about because of understanding.

There is more gratification in being a caring person than in just being a nice person. A caring attitude builds goodwill, which is the best kind of insurance that a person can have and it doesn't cost a thing.

Some people substitute money for caring and understanding. Being understanding is far more important than money and the best way to be understood is to be understanding. The basis of real communication is to understand.

Practice Generosity

Generosity is a sign of emotional maturity. Being generous is being thoughtful and considerate without being asked. Generous people experience the richness of life that a selfish person cannot even dream of.

Be considerate; selfishness brings its own punishment. Be sensitive to other people's feelings.

Be Tactful

Tact is very important in any relationship. Tact is the ability to make a point without alienating the other person.

Kindness

Money will buy a great dog but only kindness will make him wag his tail. It is never too soon for kindness because we don't know how soon is too late.

Kindness is a language the deaf can hear and the blind can see. It is better to treat a friend with kindness while he is living than display flowers on his grave when he is dead.

An act of kindness makes a person feel good regardless of whether he is doing it or it is done to him. Kind words never hurt the tongue.

Step 21: Practice Courtesy on a Daily Basis

Courtesy is nothing more than consideration for others. It opens doors that would not otherwise open. *A courteous person who is not very sharp, will go further in life than a discourteous but sharp person.*

It is the little things that make a big difference. Have you ever been bitten by an elephant? The most obvious answer is no. Have you ever been bitten by a mosquito?

Most of us have. It is the little irritants that test your patience. Courtesy is made of nothing more than many small gifts.

Small courtesies will take a person much further than cleverness. Courtesy is an offshoot of deep moral behavior. It costs nothing but pays well.

No one is too big or too busy to practice courtesy. Courtesy means giving your seat to the elderly or to the disabled. Courtesy can be a warm smile or a thank-you. It is a small investment but the payoffs are big. It enhances the other person's self-worth. Courtesy requires humility. It is unfortunate when people become obnoxious; they detract from their positive traits. I have overheard people saying with pride, "I can be pretty obnoxious."

Scatter the seeds of courtesy wherever you can. Some are bound to take root and elevate you in the eyes of others.

Manners

Courtesy and manners go hand in hand. It is equally important, if not more, to practice manners at home and not just on outsiders. Showing consideration and good manners brings out a feeling of warmth and acceptance in the home. Courtesy means practicing good manners.

Besides being self-satisfying, politeness and courtesy have many more advantages than rude behavior. Considering that, I wonder why more people don't practice courtesy. Rude and discourteous people may get short-term results. Most people like to avoid dealing with such behavior and in the long run, rude people are disliked. Courteous behavior ought to be taught to children at an early age so that they can grow and become mature, considerate adults. Courteous behavior, once learned, stays for life. It demonstrates a caring attitude and sensitivity to other people's feelings. It seems trivial and unimportant, but little phrases such as, "please," "thank-you" and "I'm sorry" take a person a long way.

Remember, being courteous will breed courtesy in return. Practice as much and as often as you can. Initially, it may take some attention, but the effort is well worth it.

Politeness is the hallmark of gentleness. Courtesy is another name for politeness. It costs a little but pays a lot, not only to the individual but also to the entire organization.

Have you noticed that sometimes when one person is telling a joke, another person will jump in and give the punch line, drawing attention to himself? And after everyone laughs he will reveal where he read it. This may show superior knowledge but it shows inferior manners.

Courtesy Shows Good Upbringing

Many brilliant and talented people have destroyed their own success because they lack courtesy and manners. Politeness and courtesy are signs of being cultured. Rudeness and discourtesy show the lack of it. Treat other people with respect and dignity.

Rudeness is the weak man's imitation of strength.

— Eric Hoffer

Step 22: Develop a Sense of Humor

Some people are humor-impaired. Have a sense of

humor and you will possess the ability to laugh at yourself. A sense of humor makes a person likable and attractive.

Learn to laugh at yourself because it is the safest humor. Laughing at yourself gives you the energy to bounce back. Laughter is a natural tranquilizer for people all over the world. Humor may not change the message, but it certainly can help to take the sting out of the bite.

THE HEALING POWER OF HUMOR

Dr. Norman Cousins, author of *Anatomy of an Illness*, is a prime example of how a person can cure himself of a terminal illness. He had a 1-in-500 chance of recovery, but Cousin wanted to prove that if there was anything like mind over matter, he'd make it a reality. He figured if negative emotions caused negative chemicals in our body, then the reverse must be true too. Positive emotions, like happiness and laughter, would bring positive chemicals into our system. He moved from the hospital to a hotel and rented humorous movies and literally cured himself by laughing. Of course, medical help is important, but the will to live for the patient is equally, if not more, important.

A funny bone could be a lifesaver. Besides, it makes life's adversities easier to handle.

Step 23: Don't Be Sarcastic and Put Others Down

Negative humor may include sarcasm, put-downs and hurtful remarks. Any humor involving sarcasm that makes fun of others is in poor taste. An injury is forgiven more easily than an insult.

When someone blushes with embarrassment, when someone carries away an ache, when something sacred is made to appear common, when someone's weakness provides the laughter, when profanity is required to make it funny, when a child is brought to tears or when everyone can't join in the laughter, it's a poor joke.

— Cliff Thomas

To a sadist everything is funny, so long as it is happening to someone else. It is not an uncommon sight to see boys throwing stones at frogs just to have fun. The boys' fun means death to the frogs. It is not fun for the frogs.

Humor can be valuable or dangerous, depending on whether you are laughing with someone or at someone. When humor involves making fun of or ridiculing others, it is not in good taste nor is it innocent. Hurting others' feelings can be cruel. Some people get their fun by putting others down. Sarcasm alienates people. It is a good idea to avoid sarcastic humor and keep it 'low-risk'.

Step 24: To Have a Friend, Be a Friend

We keep looking for the right employer, the right employee, spouse, parent, child and so on. We forget that we have to be the right person too. Experience has shown that there is no perfect person, no perfect job and no perfect spouse. When we look for perfection, we are disappointed because all we find is that we traded one set of problems for another set of problems. Having lived in the West for over 20 years, I have observed that with the high divorce rate, people find after they get married for the second time their new spouse doesn't have the problems of the first one but has a totally new set of problems. Similarly, people change jobs or fire employees looking for the right one only to find that they traded one set of problems for another. Let's try and work around these challenges and make divorcing or firing the last rather than the first resort.

Sacrifice

Friendship takes sacrifice. Building friendships and relationships takes sacrifice, loyalty and maturity. Sacrifice takes going out of one's way and never happens by the way. Selfishness destroys friendships. Casual acquaintances come easy but true friendships take time to build and effort to keep. Friendships are put to tests and when they endure, they grow stronger. We must learn to recognize counterfeit relationships. True friends do not want to see their friends hurt. True friendship gives more than it gets and stands by adversity.

Fair-Weather Friend

A fair-weather friend is like a banker who lends you his umbrella when the sun is shining and takes it back the minute it rains.

Two men were traveling through the forest and came across a bear. One of them quickly climbed a tree but the other was unable to, so he lay on the ground and played dead. The bear sniffed around his ear and left. The fellow from the tree came down and asked him, "What did the bear tell you?" The man replied, "He said, don't trust a friend who deserts you in danger." The message is as clear as daylight.

Mutual trust and confidence are the foundation stone of all friendship.

People Make Friends for Different Motives

Friendship can be categorized as follows:

1. *Friendship of pleasure.* You are a friend so long as the relationship is entertaining and fun. Pleasure goes friendship goes.
2. *Friendship of convenience.* This is where people make friends to gain something and are not lasting. There are three kinds:
   a) *Proximity*—I have my neighbour, it is convenient to socialize, we laugh together, share together. In case of emergency he is next door. It is convenient to be together. Proximity goes, friendship goes.
   b) *Usefulness*—He is well connected, financially well off, resourceful, he is a doctor, lawyer. Build and maintain the relationship, some day he could be useful. Usefulness goes, friendship goes.
   c) *Common Enemy*— There is a saying "my enemy's enemy is my friend." Common enemy goes, friendship also goes.
3. *True Friendship*—is built on mutual respect. These are people who have the good of each other at heart and act accordingly. It is based on character and commitment. There is lasting goodness at both ends. This lasts forever.

Prosperity brings friends, adversity reveals them. Fair-weather friendship is described well by the following poem:

> *Rejoice, and men will seek you;*
> *Grieve, and they turn and go;*
> *They want full measure of all your pleasure,*

But they do not need your woe.
Be glad, and your friends are many;
Be sad, and you lose them all—
There are none to decline your nectared wine,
But alone you must drink life's gall.

— Ella Wheeler Wilcox

People who are true friends in the real sense help one another, but these are not favors. They are acts incidental to friendship and never the purpose of it. If ever helping each other becomes the purpose of friendship. Purpose goes, friendship also goes.

Relationships don't just happen, they take time to build. They are built on kindness, understanding and self-sacrifice, not on jealousy, selfishness, puffed up egos and rude behavior.

Relationships should never be taken for granted. Once relationships are established, they need to be nurtured constantly. Nobody is perfect. Expecting perfection is setting yourself up for disappointment.

Friendly Cooperation

It is difficult to achieve success without the friendly cooperation of others. A pleasing personality is flexible and adaptable while maintaining composure. Flexibility does not mean flimsy or helpless behavior. It means assessing and responding appropriately and in a timely manner to a given situation. Flexibility does not stretch to principles and values.

Step 25: Show Empathy

The wrong we do to others and what we suffer are weighed differently. Empathy alone is a very important characteristic of a positive personality. People with empathy ask themselves this question: "How would I feel if someone treated me that way?"

A PUPPY

A boy went to the pet store to buy a puppy. Four puppies were sitting together, priced at $50 each. Then there was one sitting alone in a corner. The boy asked if that was from the same litter, if it was for sale, and why it was sitting alone. The store owner replied that it was from the same litter and that it was a deformed one, and not for sale.

The boy asked what the deformity was. The store owner replied that the puppy was born without a hip socket and had a leg missing. The boy asked, "What will you do with this one?" The reply was it would be put to sleep. The boy asked if he could play with that puppy. The store owner said, "Sure." The boy picked the puppy up and the puppy licked him on the ear. Instantly the boy decided that was the puppy he wanted to buy. The store owner said "That is not for sale!" The boy insisted.

The store owner agreed. The boy pulled out $2 from his pocket and ran to get $48 from his mother. As he reached the door the store owner shouted after him, "I don't understand why you would pay full money for this one when you could buy a good one for the same price." The boy didn't say a word. He just lifted his left trouser leg and he was wearing a brace. The pet store owner said, "I understand. Go ahead, take this one." This is empathy.

Be Sympathetic

When you share sorrow, it divides; when you share happiness, it multiplies.

What is the Difference Between Sympathy and Empathy?

Sympathy is, "I understand how you feel." Empathy is, "I feel how you feel." Both sympathy and empathy are important. But of the two, empathy is certainly more important.

When we empathize with our customers, employers, employees and families, what happens to our relationships? They improve. It generates understanding, loyalty, peace of mind and higher productivity.

How do you judge the character of a person or, for that matter, of a community or a country? It is very easy. Just observe how the person or community treats these three categories of people:

1. The disabled
2. The elderly
3. Their subordinates

These are the three groups of people who cannot stand up as equals for their rights.

Be a Better Person

Resolve to be tender with the young, compassionate with the aged, sympathetic with the striving and tolerant of the weak and wrong. Because some time in our lives we would have been all of these ourselves.

— Lloyd Shearer, 1986

ACTION PLAN

1. Commit to accepting responsibility for your actions.

2. Identify specifically one area in each category where you will accept greater responsibility:

   (a) Home _____

   _____

   _____

   (b) Work _____

   _____

   _____

   (c) Social Life _____

   _____

   _____

3. What three items are you committing to practice after you finish this chapter?

(i)   _____

     _____

     _____

(ii) _____

     _____

     _____

(iii) _____

     _____

     _____

Write down your commitments and read them daily for the next 21 days.

9

SUBCONSCIOUS MIND AND HABITS

Forming positive habits and character

We are what we repeatedly do. Excellence is not an act, but a habit.

— Aristotle

WE are all born to lead successful lives, but our conditioning leads us to failure. We are born to win but are conditioned to lose. We often hear comments like, "This person is just lucky, he touches dirt and it turns to gold" or, "He is unlucky; no matter what he touches, it turns to dirt." These comments are not true of anyone.

If you were to analyze the lives of the lucky and unlucky individuals being commented on, you'd find that the successful person is doing something right in each transaction, and the failure is repeating the same mistake time and again. Practice does not make perfect—only *perfect* practice makes perfect. Practice makes permanent whatever you do repeatedly. Some people keep practicing their mistakes and they become perfect in them. Their mistakes become perfect and automatic.

Cultivating a habit is like plowing the field. It takes time. Habits generate other habits. Inspiration is what gets us started, motivation is what keeps us on track, and habit is what makes it automatic.

The ability to show courage in the face of adversity; show self-restraint in the face of temptation, choose happiness in the face of hurt, show character in the face of despair, and see opportunity in the face of obstacles are all valuable traits to possess. But these traits do not just appear; they are the result of constant and consistent training, both mental and physical. In the face of adversity, our behavior, whether positive or negative can only be what we have practiced. When we practice negative traits such as cowardice or dishonesty in small events, and hope to handle major events in a positive way, it won't happen because that's not what we have practiced.

If we permit ourselves to tell a lie once, it is a lot easier to do it a second and a third time until it becomes a habit. Success lies in the philosophy of "sustain and abstain." Sustain what needs to be done and abstain from what is detrimental until this becomes habitual. Human beings are more emotional than rational. Honesty and integrity are the result of both our belief system and practice. Anything we practice long enough becomes ingrained into our system and becomes a habit. A person who is honest most of the time gets caught the first time he tells a lie, whereas a person who is dishonest most of the time gets caught the first time he tells the truth.

Honesty—or dishonesty to self and others becomes a habit: The choice is ours as to what we practice. Whatever response we choose, our thinking pattern becomes habitual. We form habits, and habits form character. Before we realize that we have got the habit, the habit has got us.

Someone once said, "Our thoughts lead to actions, actions lead to habits, and habits form character." Character leads to destiny. Form the habit of thinking right.

FORM GOOD HABITS

Most of our behavior is habitual—comes automatically without thinking. Our character is the sum total of our habits. If we have positive habits, then we have good character. Conversely, if we have negative habits, others will find our character lacking. Habits are a lot stronger than logic and reasoning. In the life cycle of habit formation, a habit starts by being too weak to be felt, and ends up becoming too strong to get out of. Habits can be developed by default or determination. If we don't *decide* what habits to form, by default we may end up with bad habits.

How Do We Form Habits?

Anything we do repeatedly becomes a habit. We learn by doing. By behaving courageously, we learn courage. By practicing honesty and fairness, we learn these traits. By practicing these traits, we master them. Similarly if we practice negative traits such as dishonesty, unjust behavior, or lack of discipline, that is what we become good at. Attitudes are habits. They lead to behavior patterns. They become a state of mind and dictate our responses.

CONDITIONING

Conditioning is the psychological process whereby we get used to (or become conditioned to) specific events occurring in association with each other. The most famous example of conditioning is Pavlov's dogs. The Russian scientist Pavlov would ring a bell each time he fed his dogs. Of course, the dogs would salivate at the sight of their meal. Pavlov did this for some time. Then Pavlov rang the bell and did not produce the food. The dogs still salivated because they had been conditioned to expect the bell with their food.

Most of our behavior comes as a result of conditioning. We are all being conditioned continuously by the environment and the media, and we start behaving like robots. It is our responsibility to condition ourselves in a positive manner.

If we want to do anything well, it must become automatic. If we have to consciously think about doing the right thing, we will never be able to do it really well. That means we must make it a habit.

When I was a student of martial arts, I observed that even the black belts were practicing block/punch, the basics, because if they needed to use these skills, they had to come automatically.

Professionals make things look easy because they have mastered the fundamentals of whatever they do. Many people do good work with promotions in mind. But the one to whom good work becomes a habit is deserving.

Good habits are hard to come by but easy to live with. Bad habits come easy but are hard to live with.

HOW DO WE GET CONDITIONED?

Think of the mighty elephant that can lift in excess of a ton of weight with just its trunk. How does an elephant get conditioned to stay in one place, tied with a weak rope and a stake, when it could easily uproot the stake and move wherever it wants? The answer is that when the elephant was a baby, it had been tied by a strong chain to a strong tree. The baby is not used to being tied, so it keeps tugging and pulling the chain, all in vain. A day comes when it realizes that tugging and pulling will not help. It stops and stands still. Now it is conditioned.

And when the baby elephant becomes the mighty full grown elephant, it is tied with a weak rope and a small stake. The elephant could, with one tug, walk away free, but it goes nowhere, because it has been conditioned.

We are constantly being conditioned, consciously or unconsciously, by exposure to:

- The kind of books we read;
- The kind of movies and TV programs we watch;
- The kind of music we listen to;
- The kind of company we keep.

While driving to work, if you listen to the same music every day for several days and if the tape deck breaks down, guess what tune you will be humming?

Insanity is defined as doing the same thing over and over and expecting different results. If you keep doing what you have been doing, you will keep getting what you have gotten. The most difficult thing about changing a habit is unlearning what is not working and learning positive habits.

THE GIGO PRINCIPLE

The computer phrase GIGO (garbage in, garbage out) is very sound.

Negativity in; negativity out.
Positivity in; positivity out.
Good in; good out.

Our input equals our output. Our subconscious mind does not discriminate. Whatever we choose to put into our mind, our subconscious will accept and our behavior will reflect accordingly.

Television has a considerable impact on influencing our morals, thinking and culture.

While bringing us lots of useful information, television has also contributed heavily to degrading our tastes, corrupting our morals and increasing juvenile delinquency. By the age of 18, a child sees more than 200,000 violent acts on TV*.

Advertisers are good at conditioning their audience. Companies spend close to a million dollars for a 30-second ad during a major event. Obviously, they are getting results. We see an ad for a particular brand of soft drink or toothpaste and we go to the supermarket and buy that brand. We don't want just any soft drink but only that brand. Why? Because we are programmed and act accordingly.

When we watch TV or listen to a radio advertisement, our conscious mind is not listening, but our subconscious is open and we receive whatever is being dumped in. Have you ever argued with a TV. Of course not.

When we go to the movies, we laugh and we cry because the emotional input has an immediate emotional output? Change the input and the output changes.

YOUR CONSCIOUS AND SUBCONSCIOUS MIND

The conscious mind has the ability to think. It can accept or reject. But the subconscious only accepts. It makes no distinction regarding input. If we feed our mind with thoughts of fear, doubt and hate, the auto-suggestions will activate and translate those things into reality. The subconscious is like a databank. The subconscious is like the automobile while the conscious is like the driver. Of the two, the subconscious is more powerful. The power is in the automobile but the control is with the driver.

---

* "As in Selling Power", *National Times*, March 1996, p. 40.

The subconscious mind can work for us or against us. It is not rational. If we are not successful, we need to reprogram the subconscious.

The subconscious mind is like a garden; it doesn't care what we plant. It is neutral; it has no preferences. If we plant good seeds, we will have a good garden; otherwise, we will have a wild growth of weeds. I'd go a step further to say, even when we plant good seeds, weeds still grow and the weeding process must continue constantly.

The human mind is no different. Positive and negative thoughts can't occupy the mind simultaneously.

In order to succeed, we need to get programmed in a positive way.

HOW DO WE GET PROGRAMMED?

Remember how we learnt to ride a bike. There are four stages: The first stage is called *unconscious incompetence.* At this stage, we don't know that we don't know. The young child doesn't know what it is to ride a bike (unconscious) nor can he ride a bike (incompetence). This is the stage of unconscious incompetence.

During the second stage, *conscious incompetence,* the child becomes conscious of what it is to ride a bike but cannot ride one himself, so he is consciously incompetent.

Then he starts learning and is at the third stage of *conscious competence.* Now he can ride a bike, but has to concentrate on the mechanics of the process. So with conscious thought and effort, the child is competent to ride a bike.

The fourth stage of *unconscious competence* comes when the child has practiced consciously riding the bike so much that he doesn't have to think. It becomes an automatic process. He can talk to people and wave to others while riding. He has reached the stage of unconscious competence. At this level, he doesn't need the concentration and thinking because the behavior pattern has become automatic.

This is the level that we want all our positive habits to reach. Unfortunately, we probably also have some negative habits that are at the unconscious competence stage and are detrimental to our progress.

NATURE ABHORS A VACUUM

I have two nephews who are tennis buffs. One day their father said to me, "This game is getting very expensive. There's the rackets, balls, lawn fees and now they have a coach. It all costs money." I asked him, "It is getting expensive compared with what?" He could have them stop playing tennis and save some money. But if they stopped, and came home from school with all their time and energy at hand, what would they do? He stopped to think quietly for some time and then said, "I think I will have them continue. It is cheaper this way." He realized the importance of keeping them involved in positive activities. Otherwise they would be attracted to the negative because nature abhors a vacuum. There is either a positive or a negative; there is no neutral ground here.

Character building becomes a habit. If we want to build a pleasing personality, we have to examine our habits closely. What begins as an occasional indulgence turns into a permanent flaw. Ask yourself the following questions:

1. Do you let the quality of your work deteriorate?
2. Do you indulge in gossip?
3. Are envy and ego constant companions?
4. Is empathy in short supply?

We are creatures of habit. That is good because if we have to constantly think before doing anything, we would never get anything done.

We can control our habits by exercising self-discipline over our thoughts. We need to harness the power of the subconscious mind. We need to cultivate positive habits during childhood which builds character in adulthood. But it is never too late to start. Every exposure to a positive or negative makes a difference. Learning new habits takes time but positive habits, once mastered, give new meaning to life.

Having an optimistic or pessimistic outlook is a habit. Habits are a matter of the pain and pleasure principle. We do things either to avoid pain or to gain pleasure. So long as the gain is more than the pain, we continue with the habit. But if the pain exceeds the gain, we drop it. For example, when the doctor tells the smoker to stop, he replies, "I can't stop! It is a habit that I enjoy!" and he goes on smoking. The pleasure is greater than the pain. One day he is faced with a major medical problem and the doctor says, "You better stop smoking immediately if you want to live." Most would stop. Why? Now the pain is greater than the pleasure.

RESISTANCE TO CHANGE

When people recognize or become aware of their negative habits, why don't they change?

The reason they don't change is because they refuse

to accept responsibility. The pleasure of continuing is greater than the pain. They may:

- Lack the desire to change
- Lack the discipline to change
- Lack the belief that they can change
- Lack the awareness for the need to change

All of these factors prevent us from getting rid of our negative habits. We all have a choice. We can ignore negative behavior and hope it will go away—the ostrich approach—or face up to it and overcome it for life. Behavior modification comes from overcoming irrational fears and getting out of the comfort zone. Remember, fear is a learned behavior and can be unlearned.

The following excuses are the most common explanations for not changing negative habits:

1. I have always done it that way.
2. I have never done it that way.
3. That is not my job.
4. I don't think it will make any difference.
5. I'm too busy.

FORMING POSITIVE HABITS

It is never too late to change, regardless of your age and how old the habit is. We can change by being aware of what needs to be changed and using techniques that modify behavior. The old adage that you can't teach an old dog new tricks is wrong. We are human beings, not dogs. Nor are we performing tricks. We can unlearn self-destructive behavior and learn positive behavior.

As Earl Nightingale said, the secret of successful people is that they form the habit of doing things that failures don't like to do and won't do. Just think about the things that failures don't do. They are the same things that successful people don't like to do, but they do them anyway. For example, failures don't like discipline, hard work, or keeping commitments. Successful people also dislike discipline, hard work (an athlete doesn't like and want the discipline to get up and train every day but he does it regardless), but they do these things anyway because they have formed good habits.

All habits start small but end up eventually being very difficult to break. Attitudes are habits and can be changed. It is a question of breaking and replacing old negative habits with new and positive ones.

It is easier to prevent bad habits than to overcome them. Good habits come from overcoming temptation.

Happiness and unhappiness are a habit. Excellence is the result of repeated conscious effort until the behavior or the attitude becomes a habit.

AUTO-SUGGESTION

What is auto-suggestion? An auto-suggestion is a statement made in the present tense, of the kind of person you want to be. Auto-suggestions are like writing a commercial about yourself, for yourself. They influence both your conscious and subconscious mind that, in turn, influence attitude and behavior.

Auto-suggestions are a way to program your subcons-cious mind. They can be either positive or negative.

Examples of negative auto-suggestions are:

- I'm tired.
- I'm not an athlete.
- I have a poor memory.
- I'm not good at math.

When you give yourself a negative auto-suggestion, your subconscious mind believes it and it becomes a self-fulfilling prophecy and starts reflecting in your behavior. For example, when a person who gives himself the auto-suggestion, "I have a poor memory," is introduced to a new person, he will not make the effort to remember the name because he tells himself, "I have a poor memory, so there's no point in even trying to remember." Of course, he won't remember the person's name the next time they meet, and will again tell himself, "I have a poor memory." It's a never-ending cycle—a self fulfilling prophency.

When a person repeats a belief often enough, it sinks into the subconscious and becomes reality. A lie that is repeated often enough becomes accepted as the truth.

Why make positive statements? Because you want to create a picture in your mind of what you want to have rather than what you don't want. Any picture that you hold in your mind becomes reality. Auto-suggestions are a process of repetition. If you repeat a statement often enough, it sinks into your subconscious mind. For example, if you tell yourself, "I am relaxed. I am cool, calm and collected," you will start responding to situations in a cool, calm and collected manner.

Auto-suggestions should not be phrased in a negative way. Don't say, "I am so disorganized." Instead say, "I am organized person." When a negative word comes in the auto-suggestion, it forms a negative picture that we want to avoid. If I tell you, "don't think of the blue elephants," it's likely that the image of a blue elephant immediately popped into your mind.

Auto-suggestions should be positive statements because we think in pictures, not in words. If I say "mother", what comes to your mind? Most likely a picture of your mother comes to your mind, and not the word "mother".

Make your auto-suggestions in the present tense. Why? Because our mind cannot tell the difference between a real experience and an imagined one. For example, parents are expecting their child to come home at 9:30 p.m. but the kid is not home and it is now 1 a.m. What is going through the parents' mind? They are probably hoping everything's okay. "I hope the kid didn't get into an accident." What is happening to their blood pressure? It is going up! This is an imagined experience. The reality could be that the kid is having fun at a party, is irresponsible.

Supposing the kid was actually coming home at 9:30 p.m. but got into an accident. What is happening to the parent's blood pressure? It is still going up! In the first scenario the imagined experience was not true. In the second scenario it was true. The body's response in both cases was identical. Our sub-conscious mind cannot tell the difference between a real and an imagined experience.

Prepare the Subconscious

Auto-suggestions can be used to eliminate negative habits and develop positive ones. We have all used auto-suggestions unconsciously. For example, when we have to catch an early morning flight, when we get into bed we tell ourself that we have to wake up at six. And invariably, we do (often, even without an alarm clock). A prepared subconscious mind works for us.

Auto-suggestion is a way to program and condition our mind to make a statement into a self-fulfilling prophecy.

Auto-suggestion is a repetitive process through which we feed our subconscious with positive statements that translates into reality. Repetition alone is not enough, unless it is accompanied by emotions and feelings.

Auto-suggestions without visualization will not produce results. The first time our mind receives an auto-suggestion, it rejects it. Why? It is an alien thought, contrary to our belief system. Success depends on our ability to concentrate and repeat the process.

VISUALIZATION

Visualization is the process of creating and seeing a mental picture of what we want to have or do, or the kind of person we want to be. Visualization goes hand in hand with auto-suggestion. Auto-suggestion without visualization is mechanical repetition and will be ineffective. In order to see results, feelings and emotions- visualization must accompany auto-suggestions.

CAUTION! Auto-suggestion may not be acceptable to our mind the first time we do it because it is an alien thought. For example, if for the past few decades I have believed that I have a poor memory and now all of a sudden, I tell myself that I have a good memory, my mind will reject it, saying, "You liar! You have a bad memory!"—because that is what I have believed up to this point. It will take 21 days to dispel this notion. Why 21 days? Because it takes a minimum of 21 consecutive days of conscious, continuous practice to make or break a habit. If you, listen to an audio tape in twenty-one days and your player breaks down—guess what tune you are humming.

The big question is: Is 21 days of conscious effort a heavy price to pay to change a lifetime for the better? Not really but only the committed do it. The auto-suggestion process sounds simple, but it is not easy. But you can do it. Follow the steps in the next section to turn your auto-suggestions into reality.

21-DAY FORMULA TO FORM POSITIVE HABITS

Translating Auto-Suggestion into Reality

1. Go to a spot where you won't be disturbed.
2. Make a list of your auto-suggestions. Make sure they are positive and in the present tense.
3. Repeat auto-suggestions *at least* twice a day: first thing in the morning and at the end of the day. In the morning, your mind is fresh and receptive; at night you deposit the positive picture into your subconscious to be working for you overnight. You can also write each auto-suggestion on a few small sticky notes. Place them in places you will see them through out the day (on your bathroom mirror, on your car's dash-board, inside your daily planner, inside your desk drawer). Seeing the notes throughout the day will cause you to repeat the auto-suggestions again.
4. Auto-suggestions alone will not work. Use visualization as well.
5. Do this for at least 21 days until it becomes a habit.

ACTION PLAN

An ounce of action is worth a ton of theory.

— Friedrich Engels

IMPORTANT: AUTO-SUGGESTIONS AND VISUALIZATIONS WILL ONLY WORK AS A SUPPLEMENT (NOT A SUBSTITUTE) TO A TIME BOUND, GOAL-ORIENTED ACTION PLAN.

1. We all have some negative habits that are pulling us down. Take 15 minutes alone and undisturbed to make a list of all the negative habits that are pulling you down.

   _____

   _____

   _____

   _____

   _____

   _____

2. Take 15 minutes alone and undisturbed to make a list of all positive habits you want to develop.

_____

_____

_____

_____

_____

3. Make a list of auto-suggestions you can give yourself to develop the positive habits listed above.

_____

_____

_____

_____

_____

4. Follow the 21-day programme with visualizations.

10

GOAL SETTING

Setting and achieving your goals

On the journey to life's highway, keep your eyes upon the goal. Focus on the donut, not upon the hole.

— Anonymous

KNOWLEDGE helps you to reach your destination—provided you know what the destination is.

 An ancient Indian sage was teaching his disciples the art of archery. He put a wooden bird as the target and asked his disciples to aim at the eye of the bird. The first disciple was asked to describe what he saw. He said, "I see the trees, the branches, the leaves, the sky, the bird and its eye."

The sage asked this disciple to wait. Then he asked the second disciple the same question and he replied, "I only see the eye of the bird." The sage said, "Very good. Now shoot." The arrow went straight and hit the eye of the bird.

Unless we focus, we cannot achieve our goal. It is hard to focus and concentrate, but it is a skill that can be learned.

KEEP YOUR EYES UPON THE GOAL

On July 4, 1952, Florence Chadwick was on her way to becoming the first woman to swim the Catalina Channel. She had already conquered the English Channel. The world was watching. Chadwick fought the dense fog, the bone-chilling cold and the sharks. She was striving to reach the shore but every time she looked through her goggles, all she could see was the dense fog. Unable to see the shore, she gave up.

Chadwick was disappointed when she found out that she was only half a mile from the coast. She quit, not because she was a quitter but because her goal was not in sight anywhere. The elements didn't stop her. She said, "I'm not making excuses. If only I had seen the land, I could have made it."

Two months later, she went back and swam the Catalina Channel. This time, in spite of the bad weather, she had her goal in mind and not only accomplished it but beat the men's record by two hours.

Why are Goals Important?

On the brightest sunny day, the most powerful magnifying glass will not set a piece of paper afire if you keep moving the glass. But if you focus the light and hold it on one spot, the paper will burn. This is the power of concentration.

A man was traveling and stopped at an intersection. He asked an elderly man, "Where does this road take me?" The elderly person asked, "Where do you want to go?" The man replied, "I don't know." The elderly person said, "Then take any road. What difference does it make?"

How true. As the Cheshire cat in *Alice in Wonderland* told Alice, "When you don't know where you are going, any road will take you there."

Suppose a soccer team is all charged up, enthusiastically ready to play a game, when someone takes the goalposts and goal lines away. What would happen to the game? There is nothing left. How do you keep score? How do you know you have arrived? Enthusiasm without direction is like wildfire and leads to frustration. Goals give a sense of direction.

Would you board a train or plane without knowing where it was going? Of course not. Then why do people go through life without having any goals?

DREAMS

Great minds have purposes, others have wishes.

— Washington Irving

People confuse goals with dreams and wishes. Dreams and wishes are nothing more than desires. Desires are weak. Desires become strong when they are supported by:

- Direction
- Dedication
- Determination
- Discipline
- Deadlines.

These are what differentiate a desire from a goal. Goals are dreams with a deadline and an action plan. Goals can be worthy or unworthy. It is passion, not wishing that turns dreams into reality.

Steps to turn a dream into reality:

1. Have a definite, clear written goal.
2. Have a plan to accomplish and write it down.
3. Read the first two twice a day.

Why Don't More People Set Goals?

The men who try to do something and fail are infinitely better than those who try to do nothing and succeed.

— Lloyd Jones

There are many reasons why people don't set goals, including:

1. A pessimistic attitude—Looking for the pitfalls rather than the possibilities.

2. Fear of failure—thinking. "What if I don't make it?" People feel subconsciously that if they don't set goals they can't fail. But they are failures nevertheless for having no goals is the sign of a failure.

3. Fear of success—low self-image or fear of having to live up to their success causes some people to fear success.

4. A lack of ambition—a result of our value system and lack of desire to live a fulfilled life. Our limited thinking prevents us from progress. There was a fisherman who, every time he caught a big fish, would throw it back into the river, keeping only the smaller ones. A man watching this unusual behavior asked the fisherman why he was doing this. The fisherman replied, "Because I have a small frying pan." Most people never make it in life because they are carrying a small frying pan. That is limited thinking.

5. A fear of rejection—worrying that, "If I don't make it, what will other people say?"

6. Procrastination—thinking "someday, I will set my goals." This ties in with a lack of ambition.

7. Low self-esteem—because a person is not internally driven and has no inspiration.

8. Ignorance of the importance of goals—nobody taught them and they never learned the importance of goal setting.

9. A lack of knowledge about goal-setting—people don't know the mechanics of setting goals. They need a step-by-step guide so that they can follow a system.

Goal setting is a series of steps. When you buy a plane ticket, what does it say?

- Starting point
- Destination
- Class of travel
- Price
- Starting date
- Expiry date

If you ask most people what is their one major objective in life, they would probably give you a vague answer, such as, 'I want to be successful, be happy, make a good living,' and that is it. Those are all wishes and none of them are clear goals. Goals must be SMART:

1. **S**—specific. The statement, "I want to lose weight" is a wishful thinking. It becomes a goal when you pin yourself down to "I will lose 10 pounds in 90 days."
2. **M**—must be measurable. If you cannot measure it, you cannot accomplish it. Measurement is a way of monitoring your progress.
3. **A**—achievable. Achievable means that your goal should be challenging, but it should not be out of reach, or the pursuit of your goal becomes disheartening.
4. **R**—realistic. If your goal is to lose 50 pounds in 30 days, you're being unrealistic.
5. **T**—time-bound. You should set a starting date and a finishing date to reach your goal.

Goals can be:

1. Short-term—up to one year.
2. Mid-term—up to three years.
3. Long-term—up to five years.

Goals can be longer than five years but then they become a purpose of life. And having a purpose is very important. Without a purpose, you are likely to develop tunnel vision where you are obsessed only with achieving your goals. Goals are more easily achieved if they are broken into small ones.

> *Life is hard by the yard,*
> *But by the inch,*
> *It's a cinch*

— Gean Gordon

Goals Must Be Balanced

Our life is like a wheel with six spokes.

1. Family. Our loved ones are the reason to live and make a living.
2. Financial. Represents our career and the things that money can buy.
3. Physical. Without your health, nothing makes sense.
4. Mental. This represents knowledge and wisdom.
5. Social. Every individual and organization has social responsibility, without which, society starts dying.
6. Spiritual. Your value system represents ethics and character.

If any of these spokes is out of alignment, your life goes out of balance. Take a few minutes to just consider. If any one of these six spokes were missing, what would your life be like?

BALANCE

In 1923, eight of the wealthiest people in the world met. Their combined wealth, it is estimated, exceeded the wealth of the government of the United States at that time. These men certainly knew how to make a living and accumulate wealth. But let's examine what happened to them 25 years later.

1. President of the largest steel company, Charles Schwab, lived on borrowed capital for five years before he died bankrupt.
2. President of the largest gas company, Howard Hubson, went insane.
3. One of the greatest commodity traders, Arthur Cutton, died insolvent.
4. President of the New York Stock Exchange, Richard Whitney, was sent to jail.
5. A member of the President's Cabinet, Albert Fall, was pardoned from jail to go home and die in peace.
6. The greatest "bear" on Wall Street, Jessie Livermore, committed suicide.
7. President of the world's greatest monopoly, Ivar Krueger, committed suicide.
8. President of the Bank of International Settlement, Leon Fraser, committed suicide.

What they forgot was how to make a life! It is stories like these that gave the readers the false impression that money is the root of all evil. That is not true. Money did not cause their problems. Money provides food for the hungry, medicine for the sick and clothes for the needy. Money is only a medium of exchange. In fact, it was the pursuit of money to the exclusion of the other five spokes in their lives that caused the downfall.

We need two kinds of education—one that teaches how to make a living and one that teaches us how to live.

There are people who are so engrossed in their professional lives that they neglect their families, health and social responsibilities. Ironically, if asked, why they do this, they probably would reply that they were doing it for their families.

Our kids are sleeping when we leave home. They are sleeping when we come home. Twenty years later, we turn around, and they are all gone. We have no family left. That is sad.

Quality Not Quantity

It is not uncommon to hear that it is not the quantity of time that we spend with our families but the quality that matters. Just think about it—is it really true?

Supposing you went to the best restaurant in town where they gave you white-glove service with cutlery from England, crockery from France, chocolates from Switzerland, and on and on. You picked up the gold-plated menu and ordered a dish of barbequed chicken. The waiter within minutes brought back a small cube of the most deliciously prepared chicken. You ate it and asked, "Is that all I am going to get?" The waiter replied, "It is not the quantity but the quality that matters."

I hope the message is clear. Our families need both, quality and quantity.

You can't mandate quality time. You can't say, "Now we will spend quality time with each other." Moments of quality come out of a larger quantity of experience. When adults were asked to recall their fondest childhood memories, they recalled moments such as their mother bringing them a cool drink and reading them a story when they were sick. Out of the time spent in mundane situations with friends and family members come pre-cious moments like sharing a joke or insight, receiving a smile of encouragement when it is most needed, or helping a friend through a tough time.

Health

If you lose your health in the process of earning money, then you lose money in trying to regain your health.

Social Responsibility

In the process of making money, if we neglect our social responsibilities and let society deteriorate, we will become a victim ourselves.

Scrutinize Your Goals

A person who aims at nothing never misses. Aiming low is the biggest mistake people make. Winners see objectives: losers see obstacles.

Goals should be challenging enough to motivate yet realistic enough to avoid discouragement. Anything we do, either takes us closer to our goal or further away.

Each goal must be evaluated in light of the following (similar to the Rotary Club's Four-Way Test):

1. Is it the truth?
2. Is it fair to all concerned?
3. Will it get me goodwill?
4. Will it get me health, wealth and peace of mind?
5. Is it consistent with my other goals?
6. Can I commit myself to it?

The following examples fail the test:

a. If a person's goal is to be the embodiment of good health with no money, it is quite obvious that it will be hard to survive. That means it is not consistent with other goals.
b. A person could make all the money in the world, yet if he loses his family and health, it is not worth it, is it?

c. A person could make a million dollars by selling
   drugs but then for the rest of his life, he would be
   running away from the law. This kind of behavior
   would be socially reprehensible, illegal and take
   away peace of mind and goodwill.

Evaluate each of your goals by putting it to the
6-question test above, and make sure all your goals are
in congruence.

Goals without action are empty dreams. Actions turn
dreams into goals. Even if a person misses his goal, it
does not make him a failure. Delay does not mean defeat.
It only means we have to revise our plan to reach our
target.

Just like a camera needs focus to take a good picture,
we need goals to make a productive life.

*Don't let the fear of the time it will take to accomplish
something stand in the way of your doing it. The time will
pass anyway; we might just as well put that passing time
to the best possible use.*

— Earl Nightingale

Goals Should Be Consistent with Our Values

Goals lead to purpose in life. It is the starting point for
success. Aim for the moon. Even if you miss, you will
become one of the stars.

*Obstacles are those frightful things you see when you take
your eyes off your goal.*

— Henry Ford

All of us in this world have a purpose in life. And
that purpose of course varies from person to person.

An orchestra would be pretty dull if everyone played the same instrument.

Make no little plans, they have no magic to stir men's blood... Make big plans, aim high in hope and work.

— Daniel H. Burnham

It doesn't matter where we are. What really matters is in what direction we are heading.

Effort and courage without purpose is wasted. Worry leads to negative goal setting. It is thinking about things that you don't want to happen.

Activity is Not the Same as Accomplishment

Do not confuse motion and progress. A rocking horse keeps moving but does not make any progress.

— Alfred A. Montapert

There is a big difference between activity and accomplishment. This was demonstrated by a French scientist named Fabre. He conducted an experiment with processionary caterpillars. These caterpillars instinctively follow the one in front of them. Fabre arranged them in a circle on the rim of a flowerpot; thus the lead caterpillar was behind the last one. Fabre put pine needles (food for the caterpillars) in the center of the flowerpot. The caterpillars kept traveling around in a circle on the pot's rim. Eventually, after a week of circling around, they dropped dead of exhaustion and starvation with food only inches away from them. We need to learn a lesson from the caterpillars. Just because you are doing something, doesn't mean you are getting anywhere. One must evaluate one's activity in order to have accomplishment.

A man was out driving with his wife and the wife

said, "Honey, we are going the wrong way." The husband replied, "Who cares, we are making great time!"

If we confuse activity with accomplishment, we could be making great time but we won't get anywhere.

MEANINGLESS GOALS

A farmer had a dog that used to sit by the roadside waiting for vehicles to come around. As soon as one came, he would run down the road, barking and trying to overtake it. One day a neighbor asked the farmer, "Do you think your dog is ever going to catch a car?" The farmer replied, "That is not what bothers me. What bothers me is what would he do if he ever caught one."

Many people in life behave like that dog that is pursuing meaningless goals.

ACTION PLAN

A good plan executed now is better than a perfect plan next week.

— Gen. George S. Patton, Jr.

1. Define success—What does it mean to you?

   _____

   _____

   _____

2. List the Goals that would lead you to success. Why are these Goals important?

   _____

   _____

   _____

3. Identify the specific goals you want to accomplish in one month, one year, three years and five years. For each goal, list smaller, specific, measurable steps you can start now to achieve them. Add deadlines to each step.

GOAL **Actions Necessary to**
Accomplish Goal Target Date

One-month

_____
_____
_____
_____
_____
_____
_____
_____

One-year

_____
_____
_____
_____
_____
_____
_____
_____

3-years

_____
_____
_____
_____
_____
_____
_____
_____

5-years

_____
_____
_____
_____
_____
_____
_____
_____

11

VALUES AND VISION

Doing the right things for the right reason

Our task now is not to fix the blame for the past, but fix the course for the future.

— John F. Kennedy

WHEN a child is born, who rejoices? The parents, relatives and friends. But who cries? The child. However, when we die, it should be the other way round. We should be rejoicing and have the satisfaction that we made a contribution to the world and left the world a little better place than we found it. Let the world cry that it has lost a good soul and become poorer.

Hindu philosophy believes that when good people pass away, they don't die. Their names live on forever through their good deeds. Recall the last time you heard an eulogy. As people pay their respects, the most common things talked about are the little acts of kindness performed by the person during his lifetime. Little acts of kindness don't go unnoticed. In fact, their impact becomes even more potent after a person is gone. That is when people realize how much those little acts of kindness meant to them.

No person was ever honored for what he received. Honor has been the reward for what he gave.

— Calvin Coolidge

HOW DO WE JUDGE OUR VALUE SYSTEM?

The seven deadly sins according to Mahatma Gandhi are:

- Wealth without work
- Pleasure without conscience
- Knowledge without character

- Commerce without morality
- Science without humanity
- Religion without sacrifice
- Politics without principle

Each of these perversions reflects a lack of values.

How do you put our value system to the test? I believe there are only two tests.

Of these the ultimate test is the "Mama Test". Whatever you are doing, at home or at work, alone or with someone—if values are in question—ask yourself, "If my mama were to see me doing this, would she be proud of me and say "Attaboy!" or would she hang her head in shame?" Your values would then be clarified rather quickly. If you passed the Mama Test and failed all other tests, you have passed. If you failed the Mama Test and passed all other tests, you have failed.

If the Mama Test doesn't do it, I have another test called the "Baba Test". Whatever you are doing, at home or at work, alone or with someone—if values are in question—ask yourself, "If my children were to see me doing what I am doing, would I want them to see it, or would I be embarrassed?" Again the clouds will clear rather quickly and you will get your answers.

If these two tests don't clarify a person's values—what would?

HOW DOES OUR VALUE SYSTEM CHANGE?

With constant exposure, what is intolerable becomes acceptable and eventually translates into involvement. As you make the transition from intolerant to involved, justification takes place.

TIMES ARE CHANGING

We worry about the declining morals of the younger generation: where will they end up? Before we point a finger at them, let's evaluate who is to blame.

Values and virtues are not hereditary; they are learned. We need to get our priorities right if we are to influence the next generations positively.

WHAT WE DO FOR A LIVING VERSUS
WHAT WE DO WITH A LIVING

Money is not the payoff for every kind of work. Parents bring up children with no paycheck in mind. **Many people have lots of money but they are very poor.** Our objective ought to be both to have money and be rich. The most unfortunate part of life is when people want to make money without earning it.

> *The best and most beautiful things in the world cannot be seen or even touched. They must be felt with the heart.*
>
> — Helen Keller

Hard work teaches a person the value of money. It is important that parents teach their children this lesson. I feel sorry for those of the younger generation who inherit money without values. Without lessons and guidance, they often equate everything with money. They think everything can be bought and sold. Of course this is not true.

CHARACTER IS PRICELESS

The movie *Indecent Proposal* brings out the point rather clearly. One act of adultery was worth a quick million dollars. People want to be overnight successes at the cost of their conscience and it still doesn't work. That's because true values are priceless. The moment a price is put on values, the values lose their worth. No possible gain can make up for that loss.

It is good to have money and the things it can buy. But the most precious things in life, money just cannot buy.

WHAT MONEY CANNOT BUY

When money talks, it doesn't always talk sense. It is not uncommon to hear that everyone has a price. People who talk that language are really up for sale themselves. People with character, integrity and the right values are not for sale. Money will buy:

- Amusements, but not happiness.
- A bed, but not sleep.
- Books, but not wisdom.
- A clock, but not more time.
- Companions, but not friends.
- Finery, but not beauty.
- Food, but not appetite.
- A house, but not a home.
- Medicine, but not health.
- A ring, but not a marriage.

THERE ARE TWO KINDS OF TRAGEDIES IN LIFE

1. Not Getting What We Want

A CREED FOR THOSE WHO HAVE SUFFERED

I asked God for strength, that I might achieve.
I was made weak, that I might learn humbly to obey ...

I asked for health, that I might do greater things.
I was given infirmity, that I might do better things ...

I asked for riches, that I might be happy.
I was given poverty, that I might be wise ...

I asked for power, that I might have the praise of men.
I was given weakness, that I might feel the need of God ...

I asked for all things, that I might enjoy life.
I was given life, that I might enjoy all things ...

I got nothing I asked for—but everything I had hoped for.

Almost despite myself, my unspoken prayers were answered.
I, among all men, am most richly blessed!

— Anonymous

2. Getting What We Want

When our value systems are not clear, getting what we want can be a bigger tragedy. The story of King Midas says it all.

THE MIDAS TOUCH

We all know the story of the greedy king named Midas. He had a lot of gold and the more he had, the more he wanted. He would spend his days in his vaults counting his gold.

One day a stranger appeared and told King Midas he would grant him a wish. The king was delighted and immediately said: "I would like everything I touch to turn to gold." The stranger asked the king, "Are you sure?" The king replied, "Yes." So the stranger said, "Starting tomorrow morning, with the first rays of the sun, you will have the golden touch."

The king thought he must have been dreaming, that this

couldn't be true. But the next day when he woke up, he touched the bed and it turned to gold. It was true—everything he touched did turn to gold. He looked out of the window and saw his daughter playing in the garden. He decided to give her a surprise and thought she would be happy. But before he went to the garden, he decided to read a book. The moment he touched it, it turned into gold and he couldn't read it. He sat down to breakfast and the moment he touched the fruit and the glass of water, they turned to gold. He was hungry and he said to himself, "I can't eat and drink gold." Just then his daughter came running into the room and King Midas hugged her and she turned into a gold statue. There were no more smiles left.

The king bowed his head and started crying. The stranger who had granted him the wish appeared again and asked the king if he was happy with his golden touch. The king said he was the most miserable man in the world. The stranger asked, "What would you rather have, food and loving daughter or lumps of gold and her golden statue?" The king cried and asked for forgiveness. He said, "I will give up all my gold. Please give me my daughter back because without her I have lost everything worth having." The stranger said to the king, "You have become wiser than before" and he reversed the spell. King Midas got his daughter back in his arms and the king learned a lesson that he never forgot for the rest of his life.

What is the moral of the story?

1. Distorted values lead to tragedy.
2. Sometimes getting what you want may be a bigger tragedy than not getting what you want.
3. Unlike the game of soccer where players can be substituted, the game of life allows no substitutions or replays. You probably won't get a second chance to reverse your tragedies.

HOW WOULD YOU LIKE TO BE REMEMBERED?

About a hundred years ago, a man looked at the morning newspaper and to his surprise and horror, read his name in the obituary column. The newspapers had reported his death by mistake. His first response was shock. Am I here or there? When he regained his composure, his next thought was to find out what people had said about him. The obituary read, "Dynamite King Dies," and, "He was the merchant of death." This man was the inventor of dynamite and when he read the words "merchant of death," he asked himself, "Is this how I am going to be remembered?" He decided that this was not the way he wanted to be remembered. From that day on, he started working towards peace. He, the Dynamite King, was Alfred Nobel and he is remembered today by the great Nobel Prizes.

Just as Alfred Nobel redefined his values, you should step back and do the same.

What is your legacy? How would you like to be remembered? Will you be spoken well of? Will you be remembered with love and respect? Will you be missed?

IT'S THE LITTLE THINGS THAT MAKE A BIG DIFFERENCE

A man was taking a morning walk on the beach. He saw that hundreds of starfish came in with the tide, and when the tide receded, the starfish were left behind on the beach. With the sun's rays, they would die. The tide had just gone out and the starfish were still alive. The man took a few steps, picked one up, and threw it into the water. He did that repeatedly. Another man came along who couldn't understand what this man was doing. He asked, "What are you doing? There are hundreds of starfish. How many can you help? What difference does it make?" This man did not reply, took two more steps, picked up another one, threw it into the water, and said, "It makes a difference to this one."

What difference are we making? Big or small, it does not matter. If everyone made a small difference, we'd end up with a big difference, wouldn't we?

IS YOUR LIFE WORTH SAVING?

 A boy was drowning in a river and he shouted for help. A man passing by jumped in the river and saved the boy's life. As the man was leaving the boy said, "Thank-you." The man asked, "For what?" The boy replied, "For saving my life." The man looked into the boy's eyes and said, "Son, make sure when you grow up that your life was worth saving."

This is a wake-up call. It is time to think.

Success without fulfillment is meaningless. Unless there is a sense of meaning and purpose, life is empty and unhappy regardless of how much prestige, money or education you have.

Success begins with developing your personal success philosophy, about your health, money, family, society and values. Without a clearly defined purpose and a philosophy to guide, life will be guided by fantasies. If we have not defined a philosophy of success, we have actually defined a philosophy of failure by default.

COMMITMENT

An integral part of a good value system is commitment. When your value system is clear it will be a lot easier to make decisions and commitments.

Example: You can't make a commitment to your country by selling secrets to the enemy. You can't keep a friend by revealing to others what he told you in confidence. You can't keep a commitment to a job by trying to do as little as possible.

Commitments not kept result in dishonest behavior. I wonder how any relationships, regardless of whether personal or professional, would work if people said something to the effect of:

- I will try but I can't commit.
- I will do it but don't count on me.
- I will be there if I can, but don't get your hopes up.
- I will be there, so long as you do well.
- I will be there so long as you are in good health.
- I will stick with you till I find something better.

If the people in the following relationships couldn't depend on one another, I wonder how anything would ever work in this world.

- Parent/child
- Student/teacher
- Employer/employee
- Husband/wife
- Customer/salesman
- Friend/friend

The uncertainty of not being able to depend upon the basic tenets of these relationships could lead to insanity. Our strongest relationships are tied together with the invisible bond of commitment. Today, breaking a promise is considered no big deal. All relationships go sour without commitment.

Lack of commitment destabilizes relationships and leads to insecurity. Where there is a lack of commitment, no one knows where he or she stands with each other.

Commitment implies:

1. Dependability
2. Reliability
3. Predictability
4. Consistency
5. Caring
6. Empathy
7. A sense of duty
8. Sincerity
9. Character
10. Integrity
11. Loyalty

If one of these ingredients is missing, commitment loses strength.

When you make a commitment to someone, you are saying, "You can count on me no matter what," and "I will be there when you need me."

Unconditional commitment says, "My behavior is predictable in an unpredictable future."

What makes the future unpredictable?

- Changes in your life and circumstances.
- Changes in external conditions.

Regardless of the uncertainty, commitment says, "You can count on me." A person who makes a commitment is willing to give up a lot. For what? The answer is pretty clear. The rewards can be priceless.

Commitment says:

1. I am willing to sacrifice because I care.
2. I am a person of integrity and you can trust me.
3. I will not let you down.
4. Despite pain, I will still be there.
5. I will not let you down in good times or in bad times.

Commitment is not like an enforceable legal contract.

Its foundation is not a signed piece of paper but character, integrity and empathy.

Commitment does not mean sticking to something when you have no choice. It means sticking inspite of choices. Without the above ingredients, no one would make a serious long-lasting commitment to others.

What makes a commitment valuable? It brings:

- Predictability.
- Security.
- Personal growth.
- Strong relationships between individuals and community.
- Lasting personal and professional relationships.

Even gangsters and crooks are looking for committed supporters. Commitment creates a patch of order in a vast tangled jungle—security in an insecure world. Keeping commitments is worth the effort. Commitment means surrendering your personal wants for another person's needs.

Keep in mind that needs are stronger than wants. Commitments act as glue that bonds relationships. Commitment implies sacrifice when required.

For example:

1. Commitment to friendship implies maintaining confidentiality.
2. Commitment to customer implies giving good service.
3. Commitment to marriage implies fidelity.
4. Commitment to decency implies staying away from vulgarity.
5. Commitment to patriotism implies sacrifice.
6. Commitment to job implies integrity.
7. Commitment to community implies responsibility.

Commitment is a sign of maturity. Commitment means not quitting at the first option or sign of problems. Individuals with strong commitments build strong communities.

Relationships are based on commitment, not just on closeness and intimacy. A person can be intimate and close, yet not be committed. Society's values have changed so drastically over the last several decades, that it is even considered good to have uncommitted relationships.

Many people confuse commitment with confinement. They are not willing to make commitments because they feel they are not ready for them. In the meantime, sometimes for years, they use anything and everything of others. Their pretext is, "We are still checking out each other before we commit." What are they checking out that they haven't already checked out in a few months or a few years?

In my opinion they are selfish parasites who are trying to get as much as possible while the going is good. They are only takers who are a liability to society.

Relationships don't last because of passion and love but because of commitment and empathy. A commitment implies putting the other person's needs ahead of one's own. Sometimes good people with the best intentions are faced with conflicting commitments. For instance,

1. A policeman is committed to caring for his wife who is on her deathbed. He is by her side when he gets a call to handle an emergency situation where ten lives are at stake. What does he do?
2. A surgeon is looking forward to his daughter's graduation. He has promised to attend this once-in-a-lifetime event. Twenty minutes before the start

of the ceremony, he gets an emergency call to operate on an accident victim to save his life. What choice does he have?

Choosing one does not mean lack of commitment to the other. The process of choosing between the two commitments involves priorities, responsibility and duty. Value based priorities help us to choose one commitment over the other, without a shadow of guilt.

The surgeon most likely would prefer to attend his daughter's graduation. But it doesn't matter what his preferences are or what he feels like doing. Commitment involves the eleven elements we talked about before, whether we feel like it or not.

Keeping commitment shows strength of character. It takes subordinating our desires to the other person's needs but not to his whims and fancies.

Needs are essential, whereas desires are infinite. And in case of conflict of needs, one has to prioritize responsibilities and duties. In a relationship such as a marriage, two people are committed to one another. Supposing one develops cancer after a year? Should one feel cheated? Deprived? Resentful? Blame the other person for ruining his or her life? That is not commitment. That is selfishness.

The most painful part of commitment is accepting a breach of trust when it happens. The commitment goes on if the breach results from an error of omission. Breach of omission can be handled with compassion and forgiveness. However, it needs evaluation if it is a result of a breach of commission. The response to a breach of commission is, "You cheat me once, shame on you. You cheat me twice, shame on me."

Commitments can rarely be kept without forgiveness.

In some relationships, regardless of whether the breach of trust is due to ommission or commission, the answer is forgiveness. For example, a child may betray his parents' trust by lying or cheating. But if the parents are to keep their commitment to the child, they must forgive him (give him direction and teach him the consequences of lying). When people betray trust just because there is forgiveness, that amounts to crookedness. Can forgiveness be treated as a blank cheque to a limitless account? Maybe not.

WHAT IS OUR GREATEST COMMITMENT?

What if we inadvertently made a commitment that is wrong or unethical and goes against our values system and conscience? Our greatest commitment is to re-evaluate whether or not to go forward with it.

COMMITMENT TO VALUES

Loyalties cannot be bought, they can only be earned. And to whom do we owe loyalties? Is it to individuals or organizations? The answer is none of them. We owe loyalties to values. Where the value system is conflicting, people cannot live in the same home or work in the same organization.

When a person makes a commitment of loyalty to either an individual or an organization, what is he really saying? He is saying, "I stand by you because I believe in what you believe in."

What if the person I am committed to, becomes a drug dealer or a spy for an enemy country? Do I continue my support because I committed earlier? Absolutely not! I am not committed to support unethical and illegal behavior.

Commitments not kept lead to:

- Broken homes
- Abandoned children
- Poor relationships
- High stress levels
- Guilt
- Unfulfilled life
- Loss of business
- Isolation
- Depression

Make a commitment and stay committed!

ETHICS

Bad circumstances are not excuses for making bad choices. Values and ethics are not just designed for good times, but also to get you through bad times. They are like the laws of the land—you need them when circumstances are good, but they're even more valuable to protect you from the bad.

Most choices are not ethical choices. For example, what clothes to buy or what TV to get are personal choices based on what is most appropriate for your situation. They are not ethical choices. Personal choices are subjective, not objective. Even though these are not ethical issues they certainly involve responsibility.

Ethical choices reflect objective choice between right and wrong. That is why your conscience hurts when making an unethical choice and does not hurt when you make a wrong personal choice—because in ethical matters there is a clear right choice. Just as with a math test, who takes it and whatever answer they give varies, but what makes it right is not the choice, but the actual correctness of the answer.

Being a nice person is not the same thing as being a good and ethical person. A person can be socially nice yet be a cheat and a liar. That makes him nice but unethical. However, niceness reflects social accept-ability. Nice does not mean good.

Unfortunately, many of our choices today seem to be based on:

1. Our desire for convenience, comfort and pleasure.
2. Our feelings—the criteria is to feel good rather than do what is responsible.
3. Social fads and ads—the philosophy that everyone else is doing it, so why shouldn't I?

It is a common belief that ethics and ethical choices are confusing. The big question is to whom? Only to those with unclear values.

SITUATIONAL ETHICS

Those who believe that ethics cannot be generalized but vary with every situation, come up with justification and keep changing their ethics from situation to situation and person to person. This is called situational ethics. This is ethics of conveniences rather than conviction.

BENCHMARKS

There's harmony and inner peace to be found in following a moral compass that points in the same direction, regardless of fashion or trend.

—Ted Koppel

Why do we have standards? Standards are a measure. One meter in Europe is one meter in Asia. One kilogram of flour is one kilogram of flour wherever you go. People who do not want to adhere to any moral standards keep changing the definition of morality by saying nothing is right or wrong, that one's thinking makes it so. They put the onus on interpretation rather than on their behavior. They feel "my behavior is okay, your interpretation was faulty."

For example, Hitler could have believed he was right. But the big question is, "Was he right?" Giving money to the hungry for food is right but at the same time giving money to buy drugs is not.

The generalization sets the benchmark; the exception is the situation. For example, murder is wrong. That is a general statement and a generalized truth and ethical standard. Unless it is in self-defense. This doesn't say that it is okay to murder if the weather is good or if you feel like it.

Our standard of ethics is revealed by the advisors we hire, the suppliers we choose, the buyers we deal with, as much as how we spend our leisure time.

Opinions may vary from culture to culture. But values such as fairness, justice, integrity and commitment are universal and eternal. They have nothing to do with culture. Never has there been a time when society has not respected courage over cowardice.

Ethics and justice involve the following:

- Empathy
- Fairness
- Compassion for the injured, the ill, and the aged
- The larger interests of society

Just because a majority of people agree on something doesn't make it right. If the citizens of a country voted to disenfranchise all blue-eyed people, that doesn't make it right. Basic ethics are pretty universal. Just as freedom without discipline leads to destruction, similarly, society without a set of principles destroys itself. If values were so subjective, no criminals should be in jail.

A society becomes good or bad, based on the ethical values of individuals. And what gives a society its strength is its underlying ethical values.

People who believe in the relativity of ethics get stuck in their own paradox. They say, "Everything is relative." The statement itself is an absolute truth. It is self-contradictory. The distinction between right and wrong, dishonesty and honesty presupposes their existence. Changing terminology does not change the meaning. Just like changing labels does not change the contents.

Low moral values become more accepted by giving them new names. The media glamorizes immorality—liars are called extroverts with an imagination.

To educate a man in mind and not in morals is to educate a menace to society.

— Theodore Roosevelt

When Michael Severn, the president of Columbia University resigned in 1993, a reporter asked him if there was any task left incomplete. "Yes," replied Severn. "It sounds complacent, but there is really only one." He referred to the lack of instructions in ethics: "The average undergraduate, however, gets no training in these areas. Most educators are afraid to touch the subject. The subject of ethics is usually left to parents to address. The result is that young people who need moral and ethical training more than ever are getting less than ever. Morals and ethics are not religion. They are logical, sensible principles of good conduct that we need for a peaceful society."*

ETHICS AND LEGALITY

Let no man be sorry he has done good, because others have done evil! If a man has acted right, he has done well, though alone; if wrong, the sanction of all mankind will not justify him.

— Henry Fielding

Most will agree that legality and ethics are not the same thing. What may be ethical may or may not be legal and vice versa. For example:

1. An insurance salesperson more concerned with getting a larger commission than selling the best policy for that particular client sells an unsuitable policy. This may be legal but it is unethical.
2. A young executive is driving over the speed limit, trying to reach the hospital with his bleeding child in the back seat of his car. Hardly anyone would question the ethics of breaking the law in this situation. It would be unethical not to get medical help to save the child's life, even if it meant breaking the law.

Legality establishes minimum standards, whereas ethics and values go beyond those standards. Ethics and values are about fairness and justice. They are not about pleasing or displeasing people. They are about respecting people's needs and rights.

---

*Adapted from John Beckley, "Isn't It Time to Wake Up?" In *The Best of ...Bits* and *Pieces*, Economics Press, Fairfield, NJ, 1994, p. 129.

PURPOSE IN LIFE

There are many kinds of desire—desire for success; desire to do one's duty even at the cost of pleasure; desire for purpose—something worth dying for which gives meaning to life.

What good is it if you gain the whole world and lose your conscience?

A purposeless life is a living death. What is *your* purpose? Do you have one? Purpose brings passion. Find or create a purpose and then pursue it with passion and perseverance.

Every day we need to ask ourselves: "Am I getting any closer to my purpose in life? Am I making this a better place to live?" If the answer is no, then we have just wasted a day of our life. Life will reward us in proportion to our contribution.

The earlier we find a purpose in life, the better our life will be. The greatest challenge lies in the unending search for the purpose of life, not only as an individual but also for our family, organizations and country. Once our purpose and values are clear, conflicts between self-interest and social obligations find a moral balance amongst themselves. We become aware of when to take a stand. That is when we start making the right decisions for long-term gain rather than making the wrong decisions for short-term gain. Wisdom and maturity lead to greater understanding of major issues.

> *Study as if you were to live forever.*
> *Live as if you were to die tomorrow.*
>
> — Mahatma Gandhi

We cannot help ourselves without helping others.
We cannot enrich our lives without enriching others.
We cannot prosper without bringing prosperity to others.

— Janette Cole, Spellman College

Janette Cole once said, "Show me a person who is content with mediocrity and I will show you a person destined for failure." Life is not a spectator sport. We cannot sit back and watch things happen. We need to find a purpose in order to make life meaningful and then strive to achieve that purpose.

LIVING WITH A PURPOSE

All of us are put on this planet for a purpose. We are part of a big picture. But very few people discover their purpose in life. Most of us just exist and keep counting our days rather than making our days count.

Dr. Albert Einstein was once asked, "Why are we here?" He replied, "If the universe is an accident, we are accidents. But if there is meaning in the universe, there is meaning in us also." And he added, "The more I study physics, the more I am drawn towards metaphysics."

I would rather fail in a cause that will ultimately succeed than succeed in a cause that would ultimately fail.

— Woodrow Wilson

FROM WHERE DO WE LEARN OUR VALUES?

I recently read the story of a high-school values clarification class conducted by a teacher in Teaneck,

New Jersey. A girl in the class had found a purse containing $1,000 and returned it to its owner. The teacher asked for the class's reaction. Every single one of her fellow students concluded the girl had been foolish. Most of the students contended that if someone was careless, they should be punished. When the teacher was asked what he said to the students, he responded, "Well, of course, I didn't say anything. If I come from the position of what is right and what is wrong, then I'm not their counselor. I can't impose my views."*

If we do not learn values from our parents and teachers, whom do we learn them from? And when they don't teach us values, we pick them up by default from television and other such undesirable sources. No wonder society gets messed up. The teacher in the example above is not only irresponsible with distorted values but does not deserve to be teaching our kids.

WINNING VERSUS WINNERS

What is the difference between winning and being a winner? Winning is an event. Being a winner is a spirit. Winners have kept winning in perspective based on their value system.

THREE INSPIRATIONAL WINNERS

1. The Olympics is a lifetime event. Lawrence Lemieux stopped racing in an Olympic yacht race to help a fellow competitor who was in trouble. The whole world was watching. His priority of safety and concern for other people's lives was

---

Journal of the American Family Association, November/December 1991.

greater than his desire to win. Even though he did not win the race, he was a winner. He was honored by kings and queens all over the world because he kept the spirit of the Olympics alive.

2. Reuben Gonzales was in the final match of a racquetball tournament playing for the world title. In the final game, at match point, Gonzales played a super shot. The referee and the linesman both confirmed that the shot was good and he was declared the winner. But Gonzales, after a little pause and hesitation, turned back to shake his opponent's hand and said, "The shot was faulty." He lost the serve and eventually the match.

Everyone was stunned. Who could imagine that a player with everything officially in his favor, with winning in his pocket, would disqualify himself and lose. When asked why he did it, Gonzales replied, "It was the only thing to do in order to maintain my integrity." He lost the match, yet he was a winner.

3. A group of salespeople left town for a meeting and told their families they would be back home Friday evening for supper. But with meetings the way they are, one thing led to another and the meeting didn't end on time. They had to catch their flight back home, but arrived at the airport with only a few moments to spare. They ran, with tickets in hand, hoping to be able to board the plane. While running, one of them hit a table knocking over a fruit basket. The fruit scattered and lay bruised all over the floor but they didn't have time to stop. They made it to the plane just in time to board. All of them breathed a sigh of relief that they had made it, except for one. He got up, said good-bye to his

friends, and returned to the table with the fruit. What he saw made him glad that he had come back. Behind the table was a ten-year-old blind girl who was selling the fruit to make a living. He said, "I hope we haven't ruined your day." He pulled out ten dollars from his wallet, handed it to her and said, "This will take care of the fruit," and left. The girl couldn't see what was going on; but as the man's footsteps faded away, she shouted from behind, "Are you God?" The salesman missed his flight but was he a winner? You bet.

One can be a winner without a medal and a loser with a medal if winning is not kept in perspective.

WINNING IS AN EVENT; BEING A WINNER IS A SPIRIT

Three people ran a marathon along with hundreds of others. None of them won the race. Does that mean that these three people were losers? Not at all. Each went into the race with different objectives. The first ran the race to test his endurance—he came out better than his expectations. The second wanted to improve on his previous performance, and he did. The third person had never run a marathon—his objective was to complete the race and he did. Each of these three entered the race with different objectives; they all met them, and they were all winners, regardless of who won the medal.

Mark Twain said, it is better to deserve an honor and not have it than to have it and not deserve it. Dignity is not in possessing but deserving.

If winning is your only objective, you may miss out

on the internal rewards that come with doing something well. More important than winning is winning with honor and deserving to have won. It is better to lose honorably than to succeed with dishonesty. Losing honorably may signify lack of preparation but dishonest winning signifies lack of character.

The real test of a person's character is what he would or would not do, if he knew he would not get caught. It is not worth compromising one's integrity and taking shortcuts to win. One may win a trophy but knowing the truth one can never be a happy person. More important than winning a trophy is being a good human being.

Winners live and work everyday as if it were their last day because one of these days it is going to be and nobody knows which one. But when they leave, they leave as winners.

There are some defeats more triumphant than victories.

— Michel de Montaigne

WINNERS ARE GRACIOUS

Winners are gracious. They never brag about themselves, they respect and appreciate their team members and opponents.

Many people know how to be successful. Very few know how to handle success.

BLUEPRINT FOR SUCCESS

I conduct a three-day seminar, "Blueprint for Success", globally, both in-house for organizations and in open public programs. The seminar is based on the philosophy *"Winners don't do different things, they do things differently."* This philosophy came as a counter to the belief *"Winning is not everything, it is the only thing."* This latter philosophy leads me to question the integrity of people who believe it to be true. It gives a distorted meaning to the words "killer instinct." If you ask a person on the street, "What is the meaning of killer instinct," most responses would be, *"You have to win by hook or by crook."* That is not killer instinct that is pure dishonesty. To a good sportsman, killer instinct means:

1. You don't put in 100%; you put in 200%.
2. To win, we must cash in on our opponent's mistake. Not taking advantage of your opponent's mistake is foolish. However, playing foul in order to win is not killer instinct, it is outright dishonesty. Unfair winning may give temporary success, but certainly not fulfillment.

The reality is that life is a competition and we have to compete. In fact, competition makes competitive people grow. The objective is to win, no question—but to win fairly, squarely, decently and by the rules.

WINNERS LEAVE A LEGACY

Great people leave something behind. Winners recognize that no one can make it alone. Even though champions get the medals, they realize that there are many people behind their success, without whom success would not have been possible—their teachers, parents, coaches, fans and mentors. We can never fully repay those who have helped us. The only way to show a little gratitude is by helping those who are following. The following poem says it all.

THE BRIDGE BUILDER

An old man, going a lone highway,
Came, at the evening, cold and gray,
To a chasm, vast, and deep, and wide,
Through which was flowing a sullen tide.
The old man crossed in the twilight dim;
The sullen stream had no fears for him;
But he turned, when safe on the other side,
And built a bridge to span the tide.
"Old man," said a fellow pilgrim, near,
"You are wasting strength with building here;
Your journey will end with the ending day;
You never again must pass this way;
You have crossed the chasm, deep and wide—
Why build you the bridge at the eventide?"

The builder lifted his old gray head:
"Good friend, in the path I have come," he said,
"There followeth after me today
A youth, whose feet must pass this way.
This chasm, that has been naught to me,
To that fair-haired youth may a pitfall be.
He, too, must cross in the twilight dim;
Good friend, I am building the bridge for him."

— Will Allen Dromgoole

Socrates taught Plato; Plato taught Aristotle; Aristotle taught Alexander the Great. Knowledge, had it not been passed along, would have died.

Our greatest responsibility is to pass on a legacy that the coming generations can be proud of.

CHANGING VALUES—TODAY'S VALUES

Change is inevitable. Whether we like it or not, it is there. We have had too much of the "me" generation and situational ethics, which have led to the loss of strong communities. People of the "me generation" feel sadness for getting caught rather than remorse for having done wrong.*

A survey of high school principals in 1958 asked this question: What are the main problems among your students? The answer was:

1. Not doing homework.
2. Not respecting property—for example, throwing books.
3. Leaving lights on and doors and windows open.
4. Throwing spitballs in class.
5. Running through the halls.

The same survey question was asked 30 years (one generation) later, in 1988. The answers were startlingly different. Here are the main problems of today's high school students:

1. Abortion
2. AIDS
3. Rape
4. Drugs
5. Fear of violent death, murder, guns and knives in school

---

* *Making Choices* by Peter Kreeft, pp. 1-2.

OLD VALUES ARE NOT OBSOLETE

A nation is held together by shared beliefs and shared attitudes. That is what enables them to rise above the conflicts that plague any society. That is what gives a nation its tone, its fiber, its integrity, its moral style, its capacity to endure.
— John Gardner

Values such as responsibility, integrity, commitment and patriotism are considered old fashioned by some. These may be old values but they are certainly not obsolete. They have stood the test of time and will be here forever. These values have the same meaning in New York as in New Delhi or New Zealand. They are universal. I don't know of any time or culture in history that did not respect these values.

VALUES ARE AT AN ALL-TIME LOW

In any society, basic immorality and injustice lead to despair. The greedy and inconsiderate who seek immoral pleasures must be stopped by those committed to real values. We have strayed in the process of change.

Any society that has lost its moral bearing is heading for disaster because all failures in history have been moral failures.

More than half a century ago, America was in the middle of a wrenching depression. One-third of the nation's wealth vanished in a matter of months. Manufacturing declined 77%. One-fourth of the labor force was left idle. Many cities could not afford to keep schools open. A fifth of New York school children were malnourished. At one point, 34 million men, women and children were without any income at all.

Yet in the depths of that hardship, with its soup kitchens, bank closings and hunger, Franklin D. Roosevelt could tell the nation in a radio address, "Our difficulties, thank God, concern only material things."*

WHAT IS GOODNESS?

If we took a survey, asking people one question, "Are you good?" most people would respond, "Yes!" Ask them, "What makes you good?" Responses will be:

- I don't cheat so I'm good.
- I don't lie so that makes me good.
- I don't steal, so I'm good.

If you analyze the above rationales, there is not much substance in them. Just think of the person who says, "I don't cheat." Well, that only means that he is not a cheat. And the person who say they don't lie and steal, only mean that they are not liars and thieves. But that doesn't make them good. A person becomes good when he actually does good rather than not doing wrong. A person of values would be one who has qualities such as fairness, compassion, courage, integrity, empathy, humility, loyalty and courtesy. What make people with these qualities good people? It is because these are the kind of people who are dependable, stand up for justice, help the needy, make life better for themselves and those around them. To recognize goodness in all its forms, we need benchmarks and standards. Benchmarks can be ethical or legal, or both. Ethical ones deal with right and wrong and all the gray areas in between. They clarify what is good and more good, and what is bad and more bad.

---

* *Journal of the American Family Association*, November/December 1991.

HOW HIGH ARE OUR ETHICAL STANDARDS?

What would you do in the following situations?

1. You know the taxi fare from your home to the airport is $64. You have paid that price several times before; you know it is the correct fare. This time the taxi driver asks for $32. What would you do?

2. You are dining in a restaurant. You ordered four dishes and the waiter brings all four but, by mistake, billed you for only three. What would you do?

3. Your best friend is terminally ill and you are a life assurance salesman. Your friend needs $100,000 worth of insurance. No one knows and no one can find out that your friend is dying. Would you write the policy?

You cannot legislate ethics. What advice would you give to your children under the same circumstances? Is your behavior in conformance with the advice you would give your children under the same situation? We start learning ethics right after birth and continue all through our lives. Can we change ethical behavior? Yes. We need ethical training.

WHAT AFFECTS ETHICS?

- Greed
- Fear
- Pressure

Pressure to perform does not justify unethical acts. To be treated fairly is not the same thing as being treated equally.

ETHICS IN BUSINESS

Ethics or lack of it is evident in every profession. Greedy doctors do unnecessary procedures and surgery. Lawyers bend the truth. Parents and children alike tell white lies. Accountants and secretaries often falsify reports.

When we cheat the people around us, most of all we are cheating ourselves. We are preparing ourselves to be cheated. Additionally, when we cheat others, we start believing that others will do the same to us and we become suspicious and pessimistic.

Prosperity brings responsibility. We cannot build industry and infrastructure while destroying the moral and social fiber.

The consequences of not following ethical behavior are the same as not following legal behavior. Some people will never be ethical. They think they are taking the easy way. In reality it is the tougher way. Could you face yourself if you didn't do the right thing for your client? Could you brag to your kids and be proud and feel good? If you can't, then that behavior is unethical.

A sense of humor and pride in yourself will keep you on course.

CONCLUSION

Why don't people achieve excellence? The big reason is the lack of vision or limited vision. We need to dream beyond what is possible. Everything that we see today was a dream before it became reality. Live with enthusiasm, direction and a sense of purpose. Do you have a dream? What is your dream? Every day that you live, are you getting closer to your purpose? Don't listen to living failures—they will give you faulty advice on how to succeed. Instead get your advice from successful people.

> *Where the vision is one year, cultivate flowers. Where the vision is ten years, cultivate trees. Where the vision is eternity, cultivate people.*
>
> — Oriental saying

Remember:

Winners
don't do different things.
They
do things differently! ™

— Shiv Khera

ACTION PLAN

... to become what we are capable of becoming is the only end of life.

— Benedict Spinoza

- Take 15 minutes to reflect quietly: What three things would you most like to be remembered for?

A _____

_____

_____

_____

B _____

_____

_____

_____

C _____

_____

_____

_____

- Now, for each of the things you would like to be remembered for, list three behaviors or activities that will move you along that path.

A 1. _____

  2. _____

  3. _____

B 1. _____

  2. _____

  3. _____

C 1. _____

  2. _____

  3. _____

Enquire about public and in-house programs from

Qualified Learning Systems
C-6/4, Vasant Vihar, New Delhi - 110057, India
Tel: 91-11-614 8804
Fax: 91-11-614 9658, 614 2656

Associate Offices:
Singapore: 124, Tanjong Rhu Road# 06–06,
Singapore-436916
Tel: (65) 6348 1954. Fax: (65) 6342 4921.

144 North Beverwyck Road # 349 Lake Hiawatha,
N.J. 07034, USA
Fax: (973) 335 7030

Please send me information on

* The seminar "Blueprint for Success"
* Keynote presentations
* In-house seminars
* Public seminars
* Audio, Video
* Books
* Bulk purchase

Name_____ **Title**_____

Company _____

Address _____

City _____ **State** _____ **Pin Code** _____

Telephone (Off) _____ **Fax** _____

E-mail: skhera@del3.vsnl.net.in
Visit us at: www.shivkhera.com

THREE-DAY WORKSHOP: "WINNERS DON'T DO DIFFERENT THINGS, THEY DO THINGS DIFFERENTLY"

Shiv's dynamic 3-day workshop entitled "Blueprint for Success" has dramatically improved productivity in thousands of people and organizations in America, Africa and Asia.

Seminar Highlights

Attitude—Ambition—Action

* Master the seven steps to positive thinking
* Turn weaknesses into strengths
* Do the right thing for the right reason
* Remove the barrier to productivity
* Introduce new vitality into your corporate culture —build trust and loyalty
* Help others to take on more responsibility
* Mutual respect to enhance teamwork
* Control things instead of letting them control you
* Become more effective immediately

What others are saying about the program:

"The best of its kind."
—**Andre Keller,** Chief Executive,
Zuellig Pharma, SDN BHD

"...stimulating, enlightening and encouraging.... I am personally and professionally enriched."
—**H John Duckworth,**
Revlon (Malaysia) SDN BHD

"Hundred per cent return on my investment is an understatement! I wish I had experienced this sooner."
—**Linda Baker,**
Certified Public Accountant, N.J., USA